CLASSIC TRAMPS IN
NEW ZEALAND

Hooker Hut and Mt Cook, Copland Track

CLASSIC TRAMPS IN
NEW ZEALAND

by

Constance Roos

CICERONE PRESS
MILNTHORPE, CUMBRIA, ENGLAND

© Constance Roos 1993
ISBN 1 85284 118 4

British Library Cataloguing-in-Publication Data. A catalogue record for
this book is available from the British Library.

Trail Maps by Hilda Chen
Profile Maps by Carto Graphics
Photographs by the author

To my father
who would have been proud

Advice to Readers

Readers are advised that whilst every effort is taken by the author
to ensure the accuracy of this guidebook, changes can occur
which may affect the contents. It is advisable to check locally on
transport, accommodation, shops etc but even rights-of-way can
be altered and, more especially overseas, paths can be eradicated
by landslip, forest fires or changes of ownership.

The publisher would welcome notes of any such changes

CONTENTS

ACKNOWLEDGEMENTS

But memories, rainbowed and fragrant
Shall linger with me to the end -
Each memory, happy and vivid,
Still keeping the mountain my friend.

A.H. Hutchinson, 1933

Since my first visit to New Zealand several years ago, I have been returning regularly to sample the splendid scenery, hike over the wild peaks and tramp through the rainforest. A paradise for the traveller on foot, from the fiords, the lush valleys, the alpine passes, to the volcanic landscapes, there is tramping for everyone, from the beginner to the expert.

I will never forget the people of New Zealand for their warmth, generosity and hospitality. Whether it be the hut warden on the Routeburn track, the ranger at the visitor station, the bus driver we flagged down on the road into Fox after finishing the Copland Track, there was rarely a brusque or impolite word and a natural graciousness that I will remember forever. Though I return home with tales of the tracks I have tramped and memories of the hills and valleys through which I have travelled, the experience of meeting New Zealanders and being permitted to share their land with them remains the most vivid.

Since our chance meeting on the Copland Pass, Jack and Barbara Coker of Dunedin have extended kindness, encouragement, and hospitality. Special thanks to Margaret Osborne, Esther Pike and Jo-Ann Reed who took me in as if their own as we tramped the Lake Waikaremoana Track in Te Urewera National Park. John Hoare of Christchurch became an instant friend and tramping companion, along with his friends in the Christchurch Over 40's Tramping Club. Dave Crow of Alpine Guides patiently guided me through Mount Cook National Park on several occasions, and shared with me his knowledge of this extraordinary high alpine land. Pat Craw of Te Anau and Liam O'Hara of Christchurch took time out to read parts

8

of the manuscript.

Many special friends back home helped as well. My uncle, Robert Shankland, volunteered his invaluable and expert editorial assistance. Hilda Chen drew the trail maps, and Carto Graphics provided the profile maps. Vicky Hoover of the Sierra Club first introduced me to New Zealand.

Of the countless numbers of trampers from other countries I met on the trail, several graciously helped with this book. Tina Cobbe and Mike Gibbs of Surrey, England, generously shared with me their video recording of our adventures on the Milford Track. Eva Zeisig of Umeå, Sweden sent her photographs.

Last, but not least, the manuscript was kindly reviewed by the following employees of the Department of Conservation: Beryl McLawrence, Wairoa (Lake Waikaremoana Track); Kerry Matthews, New Plymouth (Round-the-Mountain Track); Jan Clayton-Greene, Mt Ruapehu (Round Mt Ngauruhoe Track); Dianne Moate and Brian Gausel, St Arnaud (Travers-Sabine Loop via Mt Robert); Eric Mac Donald, Nelson (Heaphy and Wangapeka Tracks); Geoff Rennison, Takaka (Abel Tasman Coast Track); P.G.Axford, Mount Cook and Jane Welland and Chris Hickford, Fox Glacier (Copland Track); Keith Springer, Glenorchy (Mount Aspiring National Park and Wakatipu State Forest); Malcolm Anderson, Te Anau (Fiordland National Park).

Trampers in bush, Routeburn Track

INTRODUCTION

*Of the gladdest moments in human life, methinks, is
the departure upon a distant journey into unknown
lands. Shaking off with one mighty effort the fetters
of Habit, the leaden weight of Routine, the cloak of
many Cares and the slavery of Home, man feels once
more happy. The blood flows with the fast circulation
of childhood. Afresh dawns the morn of life.*

Richard Burton - 1856

New Zealand is one of the finest countries in the world to tour on
foot. This island nation's diverse and scenic wild areas make it a
paradise for the self-sufficient traveller, known variously as a
tramper, backpacker, hiker, or bushwalker.

This book begins with a general description of how best to use
it. There follow chapters on necessary equipment, general travel
information, and useful facts about time, money and weather.

Descriptions of fifteen of New Zealand's classic walking tracks,
from both the North and South Islands, highlight the book. The
tracks described are well known to those who frequent the New
Zealand bush, and are considered by many to be the best and most
popular. Each maintains a high standard of excellence for both track
and huts. They have been selected for their scenery, like the alpine
grandeur of the Routeburn or Rees-Dart, or for the tranquillity of the
Wangapeka, or for their special features, like the volcanic formations
of Tongariro National Park. Ranging from an easy stroll on the
sunny Abel Tasman Coast Track to a mountaineering adventure on
the Copland, these choices offer plenty of variety. For most of the
walks a large amount of experience is not necessary, as they follow
well-maintained and well-marked trails, with huts along the way
for shelter. A few of the tracks are only for the experienced.

Included is additional information on the geographic area of
each track, its climate and weather, and its history. Notes on each
track also provide information on nearby accommodation, available

11

tours or guiding, maps, special equipment needed, and access.

Every effort has been made to be accurate and up-to-date. But how things change: from bus schedules, to phone numbers, to water taxi operators, etc. In certain cases the companies servicing a particular area (eg., an independent bus company) have changed every year over the past few years. The actual track descriptions, however, date much less slowly than information on access, accommodation, and other support services.

Trail descriptions come from personal experience, maps, local Departments of Conservation, and just plain folks talked to on the track. Each chapter has been read by people, usually employees of local Departments of Conservation, who are intimately familiar with the track and area. Errors, however, are strictly my responsibility.

From information provided by the Department of Conservation I have recorded the approximate length of each track. Please be aware that these are, at best, estimates of distance. The best gauge to use is estimates of the time it will take to walk each section described. These are used throughout New Zealand, and recorded on some track signs. The times shown are for the average walker with a fifteen-kilogram pack, and for some will be a bit too generous. Get a handle on my pace after using this book once or twice and you'll know if you should add or subtract time when planning your tramp. None of the trips are meant to be rushed. Few of the days described are longer than six to seven hours walking and, during the longer days of the New Zealand summer, take time to stop and smell the flowers.

This book is meant to encourage people of all ages and nationalities to enjoy the New Zealand country and tracks as I have. Opportunities abound for anyone with a minimum of equipment, a sense of adventure, and a willing spirit. The rest is up to you!

Part 1: Helpful Information

CHAPTER 1: **USING THIS BOOK**

Tramping throughout New Zealand is an opportunity enjoyed not only by New Zealanders but more and more by visitors from overseas. The unique system of tracks and routes laced throughout wilderness areas and national parks provide an exciting yet safe way to venture into these remote areas. Conveniently located tough little mountain huts provide shelter and offer welcome respite for the weary tramper at a day's end. The aim of this book is to introduce the traveller to the best of New Zealand's tramping tracks. This book is meant to be a general guide only, and weather, fitness, and experience can result in considerable variation in the time needed to complete the track.

The fifteen tramps described in this book range from the easy to the expert classification. Except for the Copland Pass, they can be completed without special equipment or guiding services, and all can be reached by various forms of public transport or local private transport services instituted especially for trampers. From the array of different tramps, you may select the one that best fits your taste, fitness level, and experience.

WALKWAYS; TRACKS; ROUTES

The New Zealand Walkways Commission has set up a system for classification of the tracks. A "walkway" is well-defined pathway suitable for the average family. A "track" is a maintained and signposted trail appropriate for a fairly fit walker with some previous experience. A "route" is not well signed, and may use cairns, small piles of rocks, or poles to indicate the way, or may not be signed at all. It is recommended only for experienced and extremely fit trampers.

GRADING

A system of grading tracks and routes has been developed for this book. Tracks are rated as easy, moderate, strenuous or expert. This grading is not meant to be an absolute guide, but an approximate one, and each participant must evaluate his or her own level of fitness, health, and previous experience when deciding which track to take. If you are exhausted at the end of the day, you will not enjoy the trip. If uncertain, pick the easier trip first, and work up to the more difficult one. On all walks, you must be capable of carrying your own gear and food. Even at the "easy" level, you will be shouldering a heavy pack for several days, up and down passes, in changing conditions. Poor weather, mud, and stream crossings can slow you down significantly. You must cross passes even in the "easy" classification.

The system classification may be explained as follows:

Easy: These tracks are well-graded and maintained. There are bridges over most streams. The tracks are suitable for beginning trampers who have a fair level of fitness.

Moderate: Tracks are less well-maintained and marked. They may be rocky in places, and streams may not be bridged. Passes may be higher and more exposed than in the "easy" classification. Experience beyond the beginner's stage is required, as well as a fair to good level of fitness.

Strenuous: Tracks and routes may be only minimally maintained or not cut at all. Streams are often not bridged. Cairns and/or poles may indicate the way. Route finding experience may be required and a high level of fitness is necessary.

Expert: The tramper needs specialized equipment, and routes may not be marked in spots. Route finding experience is required and no one should attempt these tramps without a very high level of fitness and extensive previous experience.

The direction of travel described does not imply that it is the recommended direction to walk, it is just the direction preferred by the author. All tracks can be walked in either direction except the Milford Track which may be walked in one direction only, from Glade Wharf to Sandfly Point. A particular direction may be preferred for a number of reasons (ie. safety, accessibility, difficulty, elevation changes etc.). When a particular direction seems preferable, the text explains why.

Tracks in bush are marked with red and white metal "venetian blinds" on trees, or by tree slats. In general, if in open country, a track will be clearly cut and metal poles may mark the way in some areas. Cairns may indicate the correct route in rocky areas, or on opposite sides of rivers, and across avalanche gullies. The "route" designation may mean that the path is not cut or marked.

THE TRACKS

North Island

1. **Lake Waikaremoana Track, Te Urewera National Park** (Easy): Waterfalls, dense bush and a ridge walk with stunning views characterize this 51.1 kilometre track around one of the North Island's most beautiful lakes. Excellent trout fishing lures anglers as well.

2. **Round Mt Ngauruhoe Track, Tongariro National Park** (Moderate): This spectacular 49.5 kilometre tramp features smoldering volcanic craters, hot pools and fascinating volcanic landscape in the shadows of Mts Ngauruhoe, Tongariro and Ruapehu.

3. **Round-the-Mountain Track, Egmont National Park** (Strenuous): This difficult 39.8 kilometre alpine route circles Mt Egmont/Taranaki. The tramper crosses a variety of terrain from bush to scenic alpine sections.

South Island

4. **Coast Track, Abel Tasman National Park** (Easy): This 47 kilometre beach walk, appropriate for beginners and families, is more a stroll than a true New Zealand tramp. Well known for its subtropical sunny climate, golden beaches and easy boat access, it

overflows during the summer season with trampers, day trippers, kayakers and a medley of other visitors. Autumn, winter and spring bring cooler weather and less congestion.

5. **Heaphy Track, North West Nelson State Forest Park** (Easy): This popular 77 kilometre tramp crosses the South Island's northwest peninsula from Golden Bay to the Tasman Sea. Passing initially through beech forests and tussock fields, the track ends on the dramatic West Coast.

6. **Wangapeka Track, North West Nelson State Forest Park** (Moderate): This 49.5 kilometre rugged bush walk winds in and out of the Wangapeka River Valley over rough open tussock country. Considerably less travelled than the Heaphy Track, which lies to its immediate north, it appeals to the tramper who seeks solitude and isolation.

7. **Travers-Sabine Loop via Mt Robert, Nelson Lakes National Park** _(Strenuous): This loop trip is an appealing 64.5 kilometre tramp for the hardy who seek wildness yet security within the confines of well-poled and cairned routes. It offers lovely valley walking alongside swift flowing rivers combined with rocky alpine crossings.

8. **Copland Track, Mount Cook and Westland National Parks** (Expert): Requiring ice axe, crampons, and previous mountain-eering experience, the 46 kilometre Copland Track is a true mountaineer's trip. The tramper travels up a glaciated valley, over a snowy alpine pass with splendid views of Mt Cook, down the immense Copland Valley, and finally soothes his weary muscles in hot pools at Welcome Flat.

9. **Routeburn Track, Mount Aspiring National Park** (Easy): Almost as famous as the Milford Track, this splendid 39 kilometre sub-alpine tramp's easy accessibility and outstanding mountain scenery make it a favorite with all levels of trampers.

10. **Greenstone-Caples Track, Mount Aspiring National Park** (Easy/Moderate): Less popular and therefore less crowded than its neighbor the Routeburn, these two tracks form a 69 kilometre

circular route passing up two lovely quiet river valleys through beech forest with excellent fishing.

11. **Rees-Dart Track, Mount Aspiring National Park** (Strenuous): This 76.5 kilometre outing follows a river valley, crosses over a subalpine pass, and returns down a neighbouring valley. An extra day should allowed for a side trip to the Dart Glacier. Fine views of mountain ranges of Mount Aspiring National Park highlight the trip.

12. **Milford Track, Fiordland National Park** (Moderate): New Zealand's most famous walk, this 53.9 kilometre track features rain forest, a visit to the world's fourth highest waterfall, and a spectacular high mountain pass.

13. **Kepler Track, Fiordland National Park** (Strenuous): This 67 kilometre loop trip ventures into the Kepler Mountains and boasts expansive views of the surrounding fiords. New Zealand's newest track, opened in l989, is notable for its scenery, new facilities, and easy access.

14. **Hollyford Track, Fiordland National Park** (Moderate): This 55.1 kilometre valley tramp along the Hollyford Valley past Lake McKerrow out to Martins Bay on the West Coast, features views of Mt Tutoko and Madeline, the highest peaks in Fiordland National Park.

FACT PANELS

The fact panels in the appendix summarize essential information on the tramp in a succinct fashion. Much of this information is referred to in more detail in the text. This includes a general track description, total distance, time required, average total walking time, rating, starting elevation and highest point, base, maps needed, and information on huts.

TERRAIN

Short descriptions of the nature of the trail are included at the beginning of each section of the track descriptions. Descriptions such as "bush" denote heavy dense growth, "forest" for wooded areas, "grassland" for open grassy areas, "riparian" for tracks passing near or beside lakes, rivers or streams, "pass" for a gap between mountain peaks or a depression in a mountain ridge, etc. Special features described include such designations as: "coastline", "mountain views", "hot pools", "technical equipment required", etc.

TIME AND DIRECTION

All times are approximate, and one's experience, as well as fitness, should be considered when choosing a particular walk. Track conditions, weather, and elevation changes are also factors. A general rule of thumb is two and a half to three kilometres per hour but with allowance for elevation as described below. Times allow for a five-minute rest per hour, but all other stops, such as lunch breaks, longer photo stops, or the like are excluded.

Many track signs in New Zealand list the approximate time (in hours) needed to the next marker, and not the actual distance that will be travelled. Time is felt to be the best guide for planning your day since, especially to inexperienced trampers, distances can be deceptive.

Directions "left " and "right" are used to describe direction of travel with a map as reference. However, in respect to rivers "true left" and "true right" apply to the sides of a river while looking downstream.

ELEVATION

Altitude gain and loss is important when matching the difficulty of a hike to one's level of ability. A general rule of thumb in estimating length of time is to add one hour for every 300 metres of elevation climbed and one half hour for every 300 metres lost. Significant elevation gain, i.e. over 500-750 metres per day, adds substantially to the difficulty of the trip.

For each section of the tramp starting and ending elevations are given, as well as significant high and low point elevations. A guide to the trail's general steepness follows:

Extremely steep: Elevation changes greater than 125 metres per kilometre are included in this designation. You may need your hands for safety.

Steep: Elevation changes are approximately 100-125 metres per kilometre.

Moderate: Elevation changes are approximately 60-100 metres per kilometre.

Gradual: Elevation changes are around 30-60 metres per kilometre.

Almost level: Elevation changes are under 30 metres per kilometre.

Rolling: The track undulates up and downhill without significant net elevation change.

BRIDGES

New Zealanders have ingeniously devised a number of methods so that you may cross rivers without getting your feet wet. The wooden footbridge is very common. Wire covering on wooden bridges prevents slipping on its wet surface.

Swingbridges span longer creeks and rivers. Loose items or clothing may catch easily in the wires. Directions for crossing are clearing marked on both ends of the bridges. Do not exceed the bridge's maximum capacity, and do not swing or bounce.

Of other types of bridges found in New Zealand, the walkwire is the most common. With one cable for your feet, and one for each hand, they are remarkably stable so long as the wires are taut. In some of the more remote areas of New Zealand you will find a two walkwire. Take care in the wind.

River crossings are treacherous and should be approached with caution. Drownings during river crossings are not uncommon in New Zealand. Beware of rapidly rising streams that can cut off access. Keep in mind that fast deep streams are deceptive; they can sweep you away with ease. It is foolish to try to save walking time by fording such rivers simply because a bridge requires a short detour. High water routes are often options and should be used if water levels are high or trampers are inexperienced in river crossings.

HUTS AND CAMPING

The New Zealand tracks are dotted with a system of sturdy mountain huts. All walks described in this book are divided into day-to-day segments going from hut to hut. The quality of huts varies from rustic older wooden shacks to recently built, spacious structures with separate sleeping areas or sleeping shelves, and kitchens with gas rings. On the more popular routes there is often a hut warden who collects fees and keeps the premises clean and trouble free. Except on the guided tours, all the huts are self-service; you are responsible for cooking your own meals, cleaning up, and supplying your own pots or billies. In the huts without gas, you will need a cooker or stove. Stoves in the huts are for general heating only. Gas heating in huts is becoming more popular where wood supplies are scarce.

Huts are most often placed a day's walk apart - first in, first served. In some areas, especially the south, the huts provide a welcome respite and shelter from the rain. All hikers are accommodated even if (as can happen during high season) all bunks are taken. At such times makeshift beds are found on or under tables and benches and in any other available area. In my experience, such crowding occurs only during high season on the most frequented routes. Thoughtful planning, such as arriving at huts early, carrying a tent, or avoiding the most popular tracks during high season, can reduce the likelihood of this.

The Department of Conservation has established a scale of hut fees which are used to maintain and improve the huts. Category 1 huts, "Fully Serviced", often have gas, bunks or sleeping platforms, a water supply inside the hut, a stove for heating, and a warden. They may have toilet facilities. Category 2 huts, "Intermediate", are usually equipped with rudimentary heating and mattresses, and may have an internal water supply. Category 3 huts, "Basic", are smaller, older, and less equipped than Category 2 huts. Category 4 huts, "Shelter", are shelters only, have no facilities, and are free. Children under eleven are half-price. Around fifty huts in New Zealand are Category 2, and around 500 are Category 3 huts. Four hundred bivouacs and shelters are provided free of charge. Annual hut passes provide for accommodation in Category 2 or 3 huts only.

Seven of the tramps in this book are Great Walks tracks: Lake Waikaremoana Track, the Tongariro Crossing (between Mangatepopo Hut and Ketetahi Hut) on the Round Mt Ngauruhoe Track in Tongariro National Park, the Abel Tasman Coast Track, the Routeburn Track, the Heaphy Track, the Kepler Track and the Milford Track. Trampers using huts or campsites on Great Walks tracks are required to purchase a Great Walks Accommodation Pass available at local Department of Conservation offices and nearby retail networks. Passes are stamped and dated for the number of days planned. Extra days may be purchased after finishing or from Department of Conservation staff on the track. Huts on Great Walks tracks are of the highest quality. They have bunks or sleeping platforms with mattresses, water supply, toilets, heating facilities and fuel, and hand-washing facilities. They may have cooking facilities and fuel; a member of the Department of Conservation may be on duty. The Great Walks Accommodation Pass system applies to only 3.6% of the 1,000 backcountry huts managed by the Department of Conservation. However, the walks are among the most popular in New Zealand. The Greenstone-Caples and Rees-Dart tracks may be added to the Great Walks system in the future.

The Milford Track is the only track which requires a reservation, either for guided or independent walkers. Pre-payment is required through their central reservation system. A reservation system is being considered for use on some of the other very popular tracks, ie., the Routeburn.

Rules regarding camping vary from track to track. On some tracks, such as the Routeburn and Kepler, camping is allowed only in designated sites, and it is not allowed at all on the Milford Track. Camping is popular, however, on the Coast and Lake Waikaremoana Tracks, where the huts tend to be full. Camping is not allowed within 500 metres of a Great Walks track, except at a designated campsite. Campers should be careful to respect the rules of the park.

RUBBISH

New Zealand strictly adheres to the policy: "Pack it in, pack it out." Thus, you are responsible for carrying out your own rubbish. Rubbish bags may be available for purchase at Department of

Conservation offices. Paper may be burnt in the fireplaces or hut stove.

You may notice old rubbish holes near some huts. In the past they were used for all rubbish, and later filled in and covered up. In these days of heightened environmental awareness, they should not be used. The old "burn, bash or bury" rubbish days are over.

NEW ZEALAND ENVIRONMENTAL CARE CODE

> Protect plants and animals
> Remove rubbish
> Bury toilet waste
> Keeps streams and lakes clean
> Take care with fires
> Camp carefully
> Keep to the track
> Consider others
> Respect our cultural heritage
> Enjoy your visit
> Toitu te whenua (Leave the land undisturbed)

CLIMATE

The entire 1,600 kilometre length of New Zealand lies in the temperate zone, which means few extremes of heat and cold, lots of rain, and adequate sunshine. The mountain ranges make for some regional variation, especially in the South Island. Anticyclones (high-pressure systems) moving towards the east bringing fine weather, followed by low pressure systems with westerly winds and unsettled conditions. Trampers encounter the best weather between February and early April. Weather must always be a consideration in New Zealand as conditions can deteriorate rapidly. In bad weather do not hesitate to sit out a day in a hut.

HYPOTHERMIA

Trampers lose their lives each year in New Zealand due to hypothermia. Loss of body heat can be caused by cold, wind and wet clothing. The combination of the three may be deadly. Be sure to carry warm, wool or synthetic clothing, eat and drink well, have good rain gear, and do not get over-fatigued. Excessive use of cotton clothing is dangerous. Early symptoms of hypothermia include signs of cold or exhaustion, lack of interest, lethargy, clumsiness, slurred speech, or irrational behavior.

TIME OF YEAR

Most tramps in this book can be tackled from mid-November to the end of March, during the New Zealand summer. The winter (June, July and August) brings snow to the alpine passes, and the tracks should not then be attempted. High season, as used in this book, refers to the time from Christmas to the end of January. The tracks are most heavily used then and again during the Easter holiday. It follows that the best time for overseas travellers is February and March, when the weather is the driest, and the local crowds have returned home.

GUIDED TOURS

Guided tours are offered on the Milford, Routeburn, Greenstone, Hollyford, and Abel Tasman Coast Tracks. Due to the large numbers of people taken on the track, the Milford Track Guided Walk tends to be more impersonal than the other guided walks. The other tours accommodate smaller numbers, and if not family run, maintain a more intimate friendly feel. If a guided tour exists, the track description makes note of the name and location of the tour operator. Guided tours are recommended for those who do not feel confident or experienced enough to go alone, or who prefer not to carry a heavy backpack. Participants carry only their personal belongings, camera, etc. Lodging is provided in separate private huts near the public huts, along with bedding and hot meals as well as companionship. The group often consists of people from all over the world. Disadvantages are the extra cost, and a schedule that must be maintained rain or shine since another group is pressing from behind.

CHAPTER 2: **TRAMPING GEAR**

EQUIPMENT: GENERAL

Careful consideration should go into selection of your equipment for your tramp. Take a look at any mountain shop catalogue and you'll notice a confusing array of different choices, colours and prices for clothing and equipment. Equipment need not be fancy, but even if accompanied by a steeper price, it is important to buy high quality. Since safety should be your primary concern, and tramping equipment tends to take a beating, the less expensive equipment may fall apart after a short period of time. Modern manufacturers try to kept the weight of equipment and clothing down, but often this is reflected again in a higher price.

RUCKSACK

In most parts of the world, the rucksack has maintained popularity for centuries. The amount of weight you will be carrying for these trips (about fifteen to twenty kilograms if you pack thoughtfully) fits well in a top loading internal frame pack of about 4,500 to 5,000 cubic inches. The bottom can be reserved for the sleeping bag, with or without a divider to separate the bag from the rest of your gear. Although an internal frame pack is a pound or two heavier than an external frame pack of the same capacity, many find it more comfortable. Though a few people will be bothered by the pack's restriction of ventilation, the internally framed pack will stay closer to your back and move with you when you turn. Heavy objects should be packed high and close to your back.

You should carry some sort of rain protection for your pack, such as a rain cover. To provide extra insurance against foul weather, wrap all belongings on the inside in plastic bags. The New Zealand Mountain Safety Council sells a large, very strong plastic bag for lining your pack. With this heavy internal bag, my belongings have stayed dry and my rain cover became superfluous. For insurance, I still wrap items on the inside of my pack in plastic bags.

SLEEPING BAG AND PAD

A sleeping bag is necessary for all huts and for camping out, though not for guided tours. Bags with down or synthetic filling will be fine. Since temperatures are moderate, bags with temperature ratings down to -5°C or 20°F will be adequate. Your sleeping bag should be packed in a waterproof stuffsack.

Bunking in the huts makes a pad superfluous. If you plan to camp out, or if the huts are full, and you are relegated to the floor, a pad will provide welcome warmth and comfort. Down, and to some extent the synthetics now used in sleeping bags, lose their insulating value when compressed between you and the ground. I find the ³/₄ length self-inflating open-cell variety (Therma-A-Rest®) more comfortable than closed-cell foam (³/₈ inch) such as ensolite. For protection from rain and sharp overhanging branches, they should be placed inside a lightweight waterproof bag and stored inside your pack.

SHELTER

I carry some sort of shelter, either a bivouac sack, tarp or tent. For emergencies, camping out or when the huts are full, they provide essential protection.

If you prefer a tent, carry as light a nylon tent as possible, with a flysheet, some headroom, and a vestibule to protect a small amount of gear from the rain. The weight should be around two kilograms per two person tent. Modified dome tents will give you more room without too much additional weight.

Bivouac sacks, usually used by mountaineers when caught overnight unexpectedly on a mountain top, are large, lightweight envelopes of material into which you crawl with your sleeping bag and pad. They come in various combinations of nylon and a waterproof material, often Gore-Tex®. The more Gore-Tex®, the safer, drier and poorer you'll be. If you suffer from claustrophobia, it will be a long night.

Tarps come in many shapes and sizes. You may need some engineering training to rig them, especially if it's windy. Though they are lighter than a tent, the weight advantage may be lost once you carry the ground sheet you will also need. In addition, they do not provide protection from insects, and are only practical below the bushline.

COOKING EQUIPMENT

Except on tracks which are equipped with gas rings for cooking, you will need a cooker or stove, as well as fuel. Stoves in huts are for heating purposes only, and not for cooking. Kerosene is the most common fuel in New Zealand, and there are several stoves available that work efficiently either on white gas or kerosene (paraffin). Some hardware stores and petrol stations carry "white spirits" for white gas stoves, although kerosene is easier to find. You will need to carry a pot and your own eating and cooking utensils.

White gas stoves are efficient, though fuel is flammable and lighting the stoves may require pre-heating. Kerosene stoves require pre-heating and pumping, but the fuel is less flammable and safer to use. Butane stoves, often difficult to operate in higher elevations, work well inside huts in New Zealand, since elevations are low compared to mountainous areas in other parts of the world. They are the easiest to operate at low elevations, although heat output is low, and canisters are bulky and expensive. Butane/propane cartridges burn hotter and higher. Operating stoves outdoors requires the use of a windscreen.

It is a crime to take fuel of any kind, included butane cartridges, pierced or not, aboard an aircraft.

MAPS

Maps are an essential item. Learn how to read them. They are available for purchase at local Visitor Centres, Department of Conservation offices, District Infomap offices, outdoor retailers, and many bookstores.

Parkmaps are ideal for most tramps in National Parks if you stay on the track. Recommended are the maps for Fiordland, Nelson Lakes, Abel Tasman, Egmont, Tongariro, and Te Urewera. You may, however, find the scale too large. If you do, try Trackmaps of Milford, Hollyford, Routeburn and Greenstone, Kepler, Heaphy, and Wangapeka.

For more detailed maps, a metric series of topographical maps at the scale of 1:50000, NZMS 260 Topomaps, is replacing 1:63 360 NZMS 1, one inch to one mile. Providing considerably more detail than the recreational maps, they are essential if venturing off trail. Since the Parkmaps do not provide sufficient detail for the Copland Track, you'll need NZMS 1 78 Bruce Bay and 79 Mt Cook, and for the Rees-Dart NZMS 1 113 Tutoko and 144 Earnslaw.

FIRST AID

You should be carry a first aid kit. The following basics are recommended:

> band-aids
> triangular bandage
> sterile gauze or compresses
> sunburn and lip cream with high U.V. rating
> pain killers; aspirin; antibiotics
> antibiotic ointment
> safety pins; needles; razor blade
> scissors
> blister care kit
> adhesive tape at least 4cm wide
> insect repellant

TORCH/FLASHLIGHT

A torch or flashlight is helpful at night, although candles are often used for lighting after dinner in the huts. Extra batteries and a spare bulb may come in handy.

WATER

Water in most areas of New Zealand is pure, and can be drunk without concern. Unfortunately, in the last few years, contamination has become a problem in a few areas. Giardia has been found in some of the streams and rivers. This microscopic protozoan cyst has contaminated the water supply through human faeces. Hatching in the small intestine into millions of more mature trophozoites, it afflicts a sufferer with serious diarrhea, weight loss, cramps, and

27

weakness which may persist for several weeks. Warnings are posted in huts and at Department of Conservation offices.

If giardia has been a problem in the area, treating your water supply is an absolute necessity. This can be done by boiling for at least five minutes, or by using the iodine or chlorine water purification tablets available from most chemists. Also effective are water-filters designed for use against organisms as tiny as giardia.

INSECTS

The tiny, seemingly innocent sandfly strikes the unaware tourist with a vengeance. It is particularly numerous along the Milford Track (there is a section named after them: Sandfly Point), the Hollyford Valley, and other parts of the West Coast of the South Island. The sandfly herself (it is the female who bites) is barely visible, and her bite, at first, seemingly inconsequential. Several hours later the area swells, and itching becomes severe. Most active on dull grey days, before and after rain, they, thankfully, go to bed at sunset.

Several measures can be taken to try to handle them. Long sleeves and long trousers with socks tucked over the trouser legs will help. No-See-'Um ® netting should be on all tents. A trick is not to itch the bite and the irritation will last only a few days. If initially aggravated by scratching, the bites can be more than a bother for up to two weeks. Strong insect repellent with at least 95% of the active ingredient N, N-Diethly-metatoluamide, is best. Repellents with less of this active ingredient are not as effective. After you're bitten, an over-the-counter anti-itch preparation such as calamine lotion might help a bit. I treasure a lotion medication that combines lidocaine and a steroid creme. Finally, don't ignore this warning!

In some areas mosquitoes come out at night, but these are more easily dispersed with the repellent, and the bites are responsive to the anti-itch preparations.

CLOTHING: GENERAL

Though clothing requirements change a bit from season to season, the basics remain the same. Wool was considered the standard material in clothing until the last few years, when newer synthetic fabrics began to supplant its use. The old timers, however, still use wool. Wool will keep you warm when wet, as do the newer fabrics, but dries slowly. Cotton fabrics seem to drink up water, pull the heat from your body, and dry slowly. They're a poor and dangerous choice in cool weather.

The newer fabrics are most commonly made of polyester, but may also be nylon and acrylic. Known as pile, fleece, or bunting, they are referred to here collectively as pile. Pile fabrics allow moisture to travel away from your skin and keep you dry. Since pile does not retain moisture, the garments shed water and dry very quickly. Often just hanging the garment up overnight or putting your damp socks in your sleeping bag through the night is enough to dry them out. Easily layered when activity level varies, these garments will keep you warm when it's cold, and cool when it's warm. Deficiencies include less wind resistance than wool, expense, and a lack of durability. Low melting point means these garments should be kept away from high heat and even dryers.

Underwear or longjohns, often worn under shorts, are now commonly made of polypropylene or polyester which have many of the same advantages as pile, such as lack of moisture retention, quick drying and warmth. Some trampers prefer a polypropylene shirt or long underwear top to a cotton shirt for the first layer on their chest.

It is best to layer garments rather than using one large heavy item. Carry three pieces of synthetic or wool clothing for your chest. These could be a medium heavy pull-over pile or wool sweater, and two of the top long underwear, one medium weight and one lightweight. For your legs, wool or synthetic trousers plus one pair of polypropylene longjohns will do fine. Some prefer to leave the trousers behind and carry just one or two pair of the pile longjohns usually medium and lightweight. A pair of shorts and a cotton shirt may be added. Even in the rain, if the temperature is not too cool, many trampers wear shorts. Wet legs are easier to dry than wet trousers, and dry clothing is left for evening wear in the hut.

RAINWEAR

Rainwear is one of your most important items. Popular now is the alpine jacket which should be waterproof and windproof. It should fall to at least mid-thigh length, and have a hood, pockets, and sleeves that tighten. The old style cagoule or ponchos blow up in the wind and you get very wet. Jackets come in many materials. Polyurethane coatings on jackets tend to make them too waterproof but you will get soaking wet from perspiration. Lightweight nylon is useless when wet, and heavier weight nylon should still be eyed with suspicion. Gore-Tex® material is still state of the art, and, though expensive, works best. This fabric "breathes" and has much less of a tendency to condense. Gore-Tex® garments may leak if dirty, so they should be kept clean.

For extreme conditions, rain pants or overtrousers should be carried. Full-length side zippers are handy, so that they can be taken on or off without removing your boots. Despite the best protection, you will still get damp from condensation and perspiration. Remember that extra set of dry clothes you wrapped in plastic bags and left in your pack.

BOOTS

Times have changed since the days of the heavy leather boot with steel shanks. Boots of this weight provide excellent ankle support, but are excessively heavy for trips of the level of difficulty described in this book. I recommend medium weight, fully leather boots which provide adequate ankle support, but are sturdy enough for attaching crampons on the Copland Pass. They are sufficiently more water resistant than their alternative, one of the newer lighter nylon or Gore-Tex® hiking shoes. Trainers are not recommended for walking on the trails as they do not provide adequate ankle support and can, if the terrain is rocky, leave your feet bruised and sore in the evenings. Since stream crossings in New Zealand can be treacherous, it's common practice to walk right through the water in your boots and socks. Of course, boots should be well broken in before you leave home.

Two pair of socks are most commonly worn, one inner layer of polypropylene and one outer heavy layer of wool. Though some trampers wear two pair of heavy wool socks, this practice has always seemed excessive to me.

GAITERS

Gaiters will help to keep the snow out of your boots on the Copland Pass, and your socks and boots drier on the other tracks.

MISCELLANEOUS

Don't forget your southern hemisphere compass, whistle, knife, extra cord, toilet paper, pencil and paper, book, toothbrush and soap, towel, extra food, matches (in a water tight container), sunglasses, sunscreen, and one litre wide-mouthed plastic water bottle.

Spare clothing should include two to three pair of inner and outer socks, and a change of underwear. After all, if you walked through that stream with your socks on, you'll need a change for night-time. You will also need wool or synthetic hat, wool or synthetic gloves or mittens and a sun hat. You many wish to carry overmitts and a balaclava.

CHAPTER 3: **BEING PREPARED**

ENTRY REQUIREMENTS

You'll need a passport to enter New Zealand, and it must be valid for three months beyond the date on which you are scheduled to leave. In addition, you must have an onward pre-paid ticket, be in good health and of good character, and have sufficient funds to pay for your stay. Though I've never been asked to verify my bankroll, "sufficient funds" means NZ $1,000 per month or NZ $400 per month if accommodation has been prepaid. Evidence of funds can be in the form of cash, traveller's cheques, bank draft, or letters of credit. If you do not have enough money, a friend or relative who lives in New Zealand may sponsor you as a visitor.

Visas are waived for British subjects who reside in the United Kingdom. Visas are also not required for tourist or business visits of three months or less for citizens of Western Europe, Japan, Canada, Singapore or the United States, or for Australian citizens for tourist or business visits of six months or less. If you plan to stay beyond your limits, you must apply for a visa at the New Zealand consular office nearest your home.

Since entry requirements change, be sure to check on them several months before you leave home. Seasoned travellers recommend that you carry with you a spare passport photo, and a photocopy of your airline ticket and passport. If lost, they are easier to replace. No vaccinations are necessary to enter New Zealand.

CUSTOMS

You are allowed to enter New Zealand with your "personal effects", that is, articles, including cameras, which you may require for personal use during your visit. In addition, you are allowed the following concessions free of duty and Goods and Service Tax (GST): a carton of cigarettes, a bottle of "spirits" or liquor, and up to six bottles of beer or wine. For visitors, goods for commercial, business, or trade purposes up to a combined value of NZ $700,

Korokoro Falls, Lake Waikaremoana Track

Trampers and view from Mt Ruapehu, Round Mt Ngauruhoe Track
Trampers and view back to Mangatopopo, Round Mt Ngauruhoe Track

which you will not be taking out of New Zealand, are allowed. Anything over this amount will accrue duty and GST.

In an effort to prevent disease from invading its sheep, cattle, and fruit industries, New Zealand may require an agricultural inspection. Before landing, you will be asked to fill out an agricultural inspection form. Restricted items, which must be declared upon arrival, include tramping gear, dairy products, honey, nuts, fruit (fresh/dried), egg products, meat and meat products, fish (fresh/dried), vegetables (fresh/dried), plants and plant material. Its purpose is to detect any potential pests that may have secretly hitched a free ride to New Zealand. Your plane may be held up several minutes before unloading while it is sprayed to eliminate these stowaways.

Trampers are politely but carefully checked for restricted items. Food that you bring with you may be confiscated even if it is precooked and/or prepackaged. Clean your equipment, especially boots and tents, of any stray dirt and plant materials such as seeds, leaves or grass before you leave home. They will undoubtedly be inspected before you leave customs, and if not clean, they will be vacuumed. If vacuuming is not sufficient, they will be washed. This causes unnecessary delay at the airport, not to mention a soggy tent!

Officials are equally strict as well about illicit drugs of any kind. Prescription medicines should be carried in their original bottle.

TIME

Since New Zealand is located just west of the International Date Line, you'll lose a day if crossing east to west on your way over, but regain the day on your way home. The eastern shores of New Zealand are some of the first lands on earth to see the light of the new day. You'll be twelve hours ahead of Greenwich Mean Time, and during the summer when Daylight Savings Time (the last Sunday in October to the first Sunday in March) is observed the time is G.M.T. + thirteen hours. So, if it's 1 pm Standard time in Auckland, it's noon in Tokyo, 11 am in Sydney, 1 am the same day in London, 8 pm the previous day in New York, 5 pm the previous day in Los Angeles. You'll find only one time zone in New Zealand.

Since it's a long way from anywhere, you'll suffer from significant jet lag unless travelling from either Australia, Japan, the western United States, or western Canada. The farther east you begin your trip, the worse the jet lag. Night flights tend to ease the difficulty. Plan a rest day or two before starting your tramp.

DEPARTURE

There is a NZ $16 departure tax upon exit from Auckland and NZ $20 from Wellington. Although some countries permit you to claim back GST upon departure, New Zealand does not.

CHAPTER 4: **TRAVEL**

TRAVELLING TO NEW ZEALAND

A good part of the money you spend on your trip to New Zealand will go towards air fare. The number of air carriers serving New Zealand has grown in the past few years. New routes have opened up; non-stop flights have increased. With many more choices before you, it pays to plan thoughtfully.

International airports are located in Auckland, Wellington, and Christchurch. Most flights from North America arrive in Auckland. Wellington and Christchurch serve flights mostly from Australia and the Far East. If arriving in Auckland and travelling directly to other points in New Zealand, there are many connecting flights to all the major cities, and usually several flights a day to the smaller ones. Remember to go through customs in your arrival city. If you arrive in Auckland you can check in your baggage for connecting Air New Zealand domestic flights in the International Terminal. Catch the shuttle bus to the Domestic Terminal, or if, by now, you wish to stretch your legs, it's a ten minute walk.

Europe and the United Kingdom are served by Air New Zealand, British Airways, Brittania and Lufthansa. Air New Zealand, United, Quantas and Continental fly several times a week from Los Angeles to Auckland. Other airlines from North America include Canadian, Air Canada, and UTA French Airlines. Air New Zealand schedules other flights from Nadi, Papeete, Frankfurt, Tokyo, Hong Kong, Singapore, Vancouver, Bangkok, Sydney, Brisbane and Melbourne. Some Air New Zealand flights from Australia go directly to Christchurch and Wellington. Other airlines serving New Zealand include Singapore Airlines from Singapore, Japan Airlines from Tokyo, Aerolineas Argentinas from Buenos Aires over the South Pole, Garuda Indonesia from Bali, Thai Airlines from Bangkok, Royal Tongan Airlines from Tonga, Malaysian Airlines from Kuala Lumpur, Cathay Pacific from Hong Kong and Quantas from several points within Australia.

Prices vary with the time of year. The New Zealand summer is the most expensive time. In general, tickets purchased far ahead of your departure date, and carrying restrictions (charges for any changes or cancellation, limited stopovers etc.), are the least expensive. You might look at Round-the-World fares; they are often not too much more costly than round trip fares. If beginning your trip from western North America, you may wish to consider purchasing a ticket which allows for multiple stops throughout the Pacific Rim (Circle Pacific fare).

GETTING AROUND

Getting around New Zealand is easy, efficient, and reliable. Economical public transportation will take you to all parts of the country. A good network links up the various modes of transport.

Air

Within the country, Air New Zealand, Air New Zealand Link, Ansett Airlines, and Mount Cook Airline are the main carriers. All are comfortable and efficient and modern equipment is used on flights throughout the country.

On Air New Zealand National, you'll find wide body jets and twin engine jets on the major routes between Auckland, Wellington, Christchurch, Dunedin, and Invercargill. A smaller commuter line, Air New Zealand Link, connects to many other smaller cities. In conjunction with your international airfare, Air New Zealand offers a Visit New Zealand Pass which discounts airfares within the country. This must be purchased before you leave home. Don't forget to get a window seat!

In 1987, with the inauguration of Ansett New Zealand, an offshoot of the Australian airline, prices on domestic flights decreased, and the percentage of flights arriving on time, rose. Ansett flies in and out of eight cities (Auckland, Wellington, Rotorua, Palmerston North, Dunedin, Christchurch, Queenstown, Invercargill) with associated feeder service to several smaller destinations. A See New Zealander Air Pass discounts airfare on Ansett.

Mount Cook Airline, now owned by Air New Zealand, specializes in flying into the resort areas of Rotorua, Mount Cook,

Queenstown, Taupo, Wanaka, Te Anau, and the Bay of Islands. Connections can be made from Christchurch, Wellington, Nelson, and Auckland. Mount Cook Airline schedules are coordinated with domestic and international Air New Zealand flights. A Kiwi Air Pass, purchased before your departure from home, discounts air travel on Mount Cook Airline.

Don't let ostensibly high fares for domestic air travel in New Zealand discourage you. All of the airlines, in addition to their air passes, have bargain rates that can halve regular fares. Look for airfare wars between Air New Zealand, Mount Cook Airline and Ansett. Though a few conditions apply, the vacationer may find them a minor inconvenience.

Rail

Rail Services are handled through the bus company, InterCity, and you should reserve your seats, since space is limited. Though you won't set any speed records, it's a good way to see the scenery, in spite of some old and cramped conditions. The Northerner, Overlander, and Southerner, however, have been modernized, carpeted, and air-conditioned. Some trains include viewing cars and diners. Trains often run in areas with no other vehicle traffic. Cheerful commentary is provided. Bus and train services both allow you to mingle with kiwis on their normal daily business.

The following return train services are available:

Overlander	(day):	Auckland-Wellington
Northerner	(night):	Auckland-Wellington
Geyserland Express	(day):	Auckland-Rotorua
Bay Express	(day):	Wellington-Napier
Southerner Express	(day):	Christchurch-Invercargill
Coastal Pacific	(day):	Christchurch-Picton with ferry connections
Trans Alpine Express	(day):	Christchurch-Greymouth

Ferry

The North and South Islands are linked between Wellington and Picton by the Inter-Island Ferry Service, also operated by InterCity. The ferry carries passengers, freight and automobiles several times a day, and offers snack service, lounges (including a senior lounge) and cocktail bars. The 52 mile scenic voyage takes 3¹/₂ hours across the Cook Strait through the islands of the Marlborough Sounds. In high season, if you plan to take a private car across the straits, reservations must be made months ahead of time.

Ferrys run three times a week between Bluff and Stewart Island.

Coach

Coach service is extensive, with three major companies linking all sections of both islands. InterCity's network covers all parts of the country, and includes rail, coach and ferry services. Mount Cook Landline offers extensive South Island coach service, and Newmans coaches serve the North Island. Some services in rural areas are provided in small vans by an independent carrier. Often mail, produce or other goods are transported on these smaller lines. All three bus companys have their own form of discounted coach pass: the Kiwi Coach Pass (Mount Cook), Travelpass (InterCity), and Newmans Coach Lines Coach Pass. They must be purchased before you leave home. A smaller company, WhiteStar, runs a coach and freight service in selected North and South Island locations.

Coaches are comfortably equipped, tea stops are regular, and a friendly commentary is provided. Sometimes there is only one bus a day, so you should consult the bus schedules ahead and book in advance.

Recently, since the deregulation of government control over the transportation industry, many smaller transport companies have arisen. In many areas, such as on the popular Christchurch-Queenstown, or Christchurch-Greymouth routes, smaller van services now operate. Check at local Visitor Information (*i*) offices for specifics. Many of these companies offer prices well below the cost of the standard bus companies and travel the same routes considerably faster.

Some of the bus companies offer from 30% to 50% discount on regular fares for students, YHA (Youth Hostel Association) members, and seniors.

Car

Driving in New Zealand allows you the freedom you want to go where you want, when you want. Driving is not difficult, though some visitors must accustom themselves to the right-hand drive Speed limits have been increased to 100km per hour (62.5mph), but kiwis drive much faster than this. They have a remarkable tendency to tailgate, pass on blind corners, and push you over to the narrow shoulder when zipping by. Amazingly, accidents seem to be rare.

You will find motorways only near major cities. Roads are of high standard and sealed; those not sealed are well-graded and well-maintained. Roads, however, in many rural areas are narrow and twisty. You can expect to average 60-70km per hour (approx. 40mph) around New Zealand on any roads outside the cities. Progress is slowed as there are few long straight sections of road. Watch for herds of sheep heading home across the road. It's wise to stop and wait for the farmer or his dogs to clear you a path. Apart from this type of traffic jam, the country roads are relatively free of traffic.

Car rentals, handled in New Zealand by the three major companies, Hertz, Avis and Budget, are expensive. If you make a rental arrangement before leaving home, you'll save a lot. An International Driver's License or a licence issued in a major country is required. Local car rental companies are considerably less costly, but usually cannot be arranged prior to arrival. You are not allowed to take a rental car on the Inter-Island Ferry Service across the Cook Straits. Drop off your car on one island and pick up another car on the next island.

Track Access

Information on getting to the tracks is provided in the relevant chapters. Access is provided by a number of different means, such a public coaches, private local van, launch or speedboat services and the like. Look for this information at the Visitor Information *(i)* Network, Department of Conservation offices, and tramping stores.

CHAPTER 5: **FACTS FOR THE TRAMPER**

CURRENCY

The unit of currently is the New Zealand dollar which comes in coins of 5, 10, 20 and 50 cents and $1 and $2. Notes, printed in different colours with an array of native birds on the back, come in $5, $10, $20, $50 and $100.

Banks are open Monday-Friday 9:30 am- 4 pm, but close over the weekends and on major holidays. Though banks tend to have the best rates for cashing traveller's checks, they also often have a cashing fee. If holidays fall in the middle of the week, banks may be closed on the days between the holiday and the weekend. Be sure to check the bank schedules before you embark on your tramp so as not to be left short of cash on your return. International credit cards are widely accepted. Prices quoted in this book are in New Zealand dollars unless otherwise noted.

POST

Post offices are generally open from 8:30 am to 5 pm weekdays, and until 8 pm on Fridays. Mail delivery within New Zealand takes two to three days and costs $.45 for a postcard or a letter. "Across town" delivery is posted by the next working day. Next day delivery within New Zealand (Fastpost) costs $.80. Delivery to and from a few remote areas may take a little longer. Mail should be posted by 5 pm weekdays.

Overseas mail is relatively expensive. Surface international mail (global rates) anywhere in the world costs $.50 for a postcard and $.65 for a letter. Airmail (Fastpost) postcards around the world cost $1.00. Airmail letters to Australia and the rest of the South Pacific are $1.00, to North America and Asia (excluding the Middle East) $1.50, and to Europe, South America, Africa and the Middle East $1.80. Overseas airmail delivery can take up to twelve days, and surface mail up to ten weeks. Surface air delivery, available for parcels only, takes three to six weeks.

Mail from home may be addressed to yourself at the CPO (Chief

Post Office) in any town, and your letters will be held for a month. Telephones can be found at many post offices.

GOODS AND SERVICE TAX

Inflation has hit New Zealand hard, especially since the 1986 inauguration of the GST (Goods and Service Tax), which added 12.5% to just about everything. Most prices are quoted inclusive of GST, but get ready for a shock when one is not.

TELEPHONES

A local call from a pay phone costs $.20. Calls beyond the local area can be expensive requiring large numbers of coins. Card phones make the process considerably easier. Purchased in denominations of $5, $10, $20 and $50, the cards are inserted in a slot in the phone and the cost of the call is deducted electronically. You should have a second card ready for use if the money runs out on the first. Calls are cut off until a valid card in inserted. Finding a card phone when you have a card, and a coin phone when you wish to use coins, is not always easy. You may also make calls at Telecom, the phone company offices, or at a post office, and these you can pay for afterwards.

International calls are most easily made with an international calling card, and if you use a pay phone, there is no surcharge. Hotels, motels or Telecom do, however, often add a surcharge.

A service from Telecom, NZ Direct, allows overseas travellers to make collect calls home using a Telecom International Operator. Telecom provides leaflets describing this service.

Dial 111 for emergency, 018 for Directory Assistance, 0170 for International Operator Service, and 0172 for International Directory Assistance.

TIPPING

Kiwis don't do it, so why should you? The feeling is that everyone earns a good living and needs no bonuses. It may be hard to resist the urge. You can be sure that, tip or no tip, you will get the same gracious friendly service everywhere.

HOLIDAYS

New Zealanders love holidays and it's a grand excuse for just about everyone to head off to the lake, the beach, or for a tramping area. Resorts are overcrowded during these periods. They are also busy during school holidays from Christmas to the beginning of February, on the Waitangi Day holiday, and over the Easter weekend. There are also two-week school holidays in May and August.

National Public Holidays are:

1 January :	New Year's Day
2 January :	New Year's Holiday
6 February:	Waitangi Day or New Zealand Day (the day the Treaty of Waitangi was signed)
March/April:	Good Friday, Easter, and Easter Monday
25 April:	ANZAC Day (the day Australian and New Zealand troops landed in Gallipoli in 1915)
June (first Monday)	Queen's Birthday
October (last Monday)	Labour Day
25 December	Christmas
26 December	Boxing Day

CHAPTER 6: **WHERE TO STAY**

An array of accommodation is available throughout New Zealand. The choice extends from luxury hotels, motels, bed-and-breakfasts or guesthouses, to hostels and backpacker's lodges. In the some of the cities or sizeable towns, such as Nelson, Queenstown and Te Anau, and in certain smaller tourist centres such as Mount Cook or National Park/Whakapapa Village, the selection covers the complete range. In other areas, such as St Arnaud (Nelson Lakes National Park) or Lake Waikaremoana (Te Urewera National Park) there is a limited choice. Upon your arrival, the Visitor Information Network, easily identified by "*i* ", has booths at both Auckland and Christchurch International Airports. They have very useful literature covering all levels of accommodation throughout the country.

All accommodation shares some common features. All provide access to an electric kettle, sugar, tea, coffee, and milk in your room or in a centrally located public area. Telephones are also available. If laundry facilities are absent, there is always some means of getting your washing done for you.

YOUTH HOSTELS/BACKPACKERS

Youth hostels and backpacker's accommodation is the least expensive. You'll find visitors of all ages, from New Zealand and overseas. When travelling alone, it's a great way to meet other people, and perhaps find a new travelling companion. The number of hostels and backpacker's lodges has increased in recent years in response to an increase in travellers wanting budget accommodation. In general, you will find these lodges to be clean and of good quality. Although a few of the hostels have two-bed or single rooms, most provide bunkrooms segregated by sex. Hostels run by YHA (Youth Hostel Association) require that you be a member. You can join at home, in Auckland or Christchurch, or at the hostel itself. At the Visitor Information (*i*) Network look for New Zealand Hostel Association's *Good Bed Guide*, a directory of the country's youth hostels.

All hostels have communal sitting rooms, hot showers, kitchens, and laundry facilities. Bring your own sleeping bag and cooking utensils.

MOTOR CAMPS

Motor camps appeal to trampers and campers alike, especially those watching their expenses. Conveniently located just about everywhere, in cities and remote places as well, they provide a choice among tent sites, caravan sites, bunkhouses, and cabins. Some of the motor camps have spacious grounds in lakeside or mountain locations. Toilets, showers, laundry and cooking areas, if not in your individual unit, are centrally located. Bring your own food, sleeping bag or blankets (you often can rent them) and cooking utensils. The premises usually include a small store with some supplies.

BED AND BREAKFASTS/GUESTHOUSES

Moderately priced bed and breakfast/guesthouse accommodation offer the traveller quite a bit more than the less expensive hostels or backpacker's accommodation. They are usually situated in well-restored older homes or buildings. Owner occupied, and tended with great care, they are comfortable and clean, and offer a personal touch missing from some motels and hotels. They all provide a full breakfast; a few serve dinner. A common area allows you to meet and chat with other travellers. Rooms are private, but often the bathroom is down the hall. A private bath costs extra. Owners are usually very happy to advise their guests on local tours and sightseeing. Some of these establishments are listed in a brochure provided by the New Zealand Travel Hotels/Motels Federation Inc.

MOTELS

New Zealand's motels differ a bit from motels in other parts of the world. They do not cater exclusively to motor traffic. A fully equipped unit with a refrigerator, tea and coffee supplies, full kitchen and private bath or shower, is provided. Some of the units have two bedrooms and a central lounge with an adjoining bathroom. Many of the motels are owner occupied. They tend to be in the centre of town, so just walk right in if you don't have a car. The only drawback is that some lack certain services. During a stay of more than one night, you may find yourself doing your own housekeeping.

HOTELS

Hotels in New Zealand, much costlier than the other types of accommodation, give you a broad range of facilities and services. All hotels are licensed to serve alcohol, and a restaurant is often attached. In the larger cities of Auckland, Wellington and Christchurch, you will find world class hotels. The more moderately priced hotels also offer plenty of services, but standards may vary.

In rural towns, especially on the South Island's West Coast, the one small hotel is often the centre of local social life, with the pub being the most important room. Here you can enjoy a true kiwi-style dinner. Though these country hotels may be older than the urban type, they are well cared for, and hold to the high standards of cleanliness you will find typical of New Zealand.

CONTACTS

New Zealand Travel Hotels/Motels Federation Inc., 52 Armagh
    Street, Christchurch,   0-3-661 1503
Youth Hostel Association of New Zealand National Office,
    PO Box 436, Christchurch,   0-3-379 9970

YHA Travel Centres:
Christchurch: Cnr 36 Customs St and Gore St   0-3-379 9970
Auckland: Cnr Gloucester St and Manchester St   0-9-379 4224

Visitor Information *(i)* Network:
Auckland International Airport, International and Domestic
Terminals: 0-9-275 0789
    Aotea Square   0-9-366 6888
Christchurch International Airport, Domestic Terminal:
                              0-3-353 0783
    Cnr Worcester and Oxford St   0-3-379 9629

Welcome Flat Hut, Copland Track

Part 2: The Tracks

NORTH ISLAND

Track	Location	Distance km	Time days	Rating	Base
Lake Waikaremoana	Te Urewera Natl Park	51.1	3-5	Easy	Aniwaniwa Visitor Centre
Round Mt Ngauruhoe	Tongariro Natl Park	49.5	3-4	Mod	Whakapapa Village
Round-the-Mountain	Egmont Natl Park	39.8	3-4	Stren	New Plymouth

SOUTH ISLAND

Track	Location	Distance km	Time days	Rating	Base
Coast	Abel Tasman Natl Park	47.0	3-5	Easy	Nelson
Heaphy	North West Nelson State Forest Park	77.0	4-5	Easy	Nelson
Wangapeka	North West Nelson State Forest Park	49.5	4-5	Stren	Nelson/ Karamea
Travers-Sabine	Nelson Lakes Natl Park	64.5	6-7	Stren	St Arnaud
Copland	Mount Cook Natl Park Westland Natl Park	46.0	3-4	Expert	Mount Cook Village

Track	Location	Distance km	Time days	Rating	Base
Routeburn	Mount Aspiring Natl Park	39.0	2-3	Easy	Te Anau/ Queenstown
Greenstone	Wakatipu State Forest	36.5	2	Easy	Queenstown
Caples	Wakatipu State Forest	32.5	2	Mod	Queenstown
Rees-Dart	Mount Aspiring Natl Park	76.5	4-5	Stren	Queenstown
Milford	Fiordland Natl Park	53.9	4	Mod	Te Anau
Kepler	Fiordland Natl Park	67.0	3-4	Stren	Te Anau
Hollyford	Fiordland Natl Park	55.1	4	Mod	Te Anau

(See also Summary Tables- appendix pp.197 - 207)

CHAPTER 7: **NORTH ISLAND, EAST: TE UREWERA NATIONAL PARK**

LAKE WAIKAREMOANA TRACK

As long as I live, I'll hear waterfalls and birds sing.
I'll interpret the rocks, learn the language of flood,
storm, and avalanche.
I'll acquaint myself with the glaciers and wild gardens
and get as near the heart of the world as I can.

John Muir

In Te Urewera National Park, the Lake Track circles Lake Waikaremoana, considered one of the North Island's most beautiful lakes. All botanical features characteristic of the North Island find a place here: dense forest, river flats, trout filled waters, and rushing streams with waterfalls. Bush encloses the tramper during much of the walk with occasional breaks for views of the lake. The only time the tramper leaves the lake level is for the climb up to Panekiri bluffs where sweeping vistas reward the climber.

The Maori influence is strong in this area, and as one winds around the tortuous shores of the lake, a sense of their history pervades. Legends interlace with the trees and rivers and add a mystery and fascination to the land. As the legend relates, a Maori chief drowned his disobedient daughter in the lake. In her attempts to escape, she called on the Gods who turned her into a taniwha (water dragon). In her efforts to reach safety, she gouged out the arms of the Lake. Her efforts failed and she turned into stone. She now lies in Waikaretaheke Stream - the only outlet to the Lake. From the force of her attempts, the Lake was formed and named Waikaremoana "the sea of rippling waters".

WEATHER

The high nature of this mountainous area leads to rainfall up to 2500 millimetres per year, significantly higher than in either of the surrounding areas of Napier or Rotorua. Fog and mist, distinguishing features of the park, are common in the early morning hours. Late summer and early autumn may bring long spells of warm weather, and snow sometimes falls in winter at the higher elevations.

BASE

In the centre of the park, two kilometres from the Aniwaniwa Visitor Centre, a convenient starting point is the motor camp at Lake Waikaremoana, which provides cabins, a bunkhouse, a camping area and a small store with limited supplies. For a small fee, you may park your car here and pick up public transport to either end of the track. Additional accommodation includes a motel at Ruatahuna and camping areas at Mokau, Hopuruahine, Aniwaniwa and Rosie Bay. At the Aniwaniwa Visitor Centre, you may pay for your Great Walks Pass, get up-to-date track information and view the displays.

HISTORY

The area was traditionally inhabited by the Maori Tuhoe and Ruapani tribes. Records of their presence go back to the fourteenth century, but they remained isolated from the rest of the country until the second decade of the twentieth century. They were a fierce tribe fighting for independence from neighbouring tribes, and the Tuhoe influence persists to this day.

The area seemed so rugged and inhospitable to the early European explorers, that they made no attempt to settle. Thus, the tribes remained isolated. A couple of decades later, the Europeans decided to inhabit the area, and eventually overcame the tribes.

In 1895, the first road into the park between Murupara and Ruatahuna was begun. State Highway 38, connecting Rotorua with Wairoa, cuts through the centre of the park, and today is still windy and unsealed. Although efforts to preserve the area began as early as 1925, national park status did not come until 1954. The track was started in 1962 as a volunteer project by boys from fourteen secondary schools.

TRANSPORT/TRACK ACCESS

The main access road through the park, connecting Murupara with Wairoa, is State Highway 38 which meets Highway 5 about 20 minutes south of Rotorua. From Murupara, where there is a motor camp, the trip to Park Headquarters is about 2 hours (100 kilometres) on unsealed winding road, and another hour (63 kilometres) to Wairoa, although the road is improved just after Onepoto, 20 minutes after the Visitor Centre. Wairoa is 119 kilometres NE of Napier and 93 kilometres SW of Gisborne.

Napier and Rotorua are served by InterCity and Newmans bus services. InterCity has connecting bus services from Napier to Wairoa. Rotorua and Napier may be reached by Air New Zealand Link or Mount Cook Airlines. Train service serves the Wellington-Napier route, and Auckland-Rotorua route.

Local van services, the City Connection, from Wairoa to Rotorua and return, pass through the park three days a week and stop at the Waikaremoana Motor Camp, Aniwaniwa Visitor Centre and at both ends of the track. The City Connection connects with the train from Auckland. There is also boat and bus service operating from Tuai, where you may safely leave your car. Twice a day from mid-December to the end of January, and during Easter week, the boat or bus service starts from Onepoto, goes to the Motor Camp and on to Hopuruahine Landing and return. On demand service is available the rest of the year.

THE TRACK

One of the best known tracks on the North Island, the Lake Track is 51.1 kilometres long with five nicely spaced huts along the way. The groomed, well-marked track may be walked in either direction, and is rated easy, the only difficult section being the climb over and down from Panekiri Bluffs. The walk will be described starting from Hopuruahine Landing, which leaves the most magnificent views and most pleasant hut until the last day. Many, however, prefer to start from the Onepoto end because the climb up to Panekiri Bluffs is gentler than if starting the ascent from the Waiopaoa Hut.

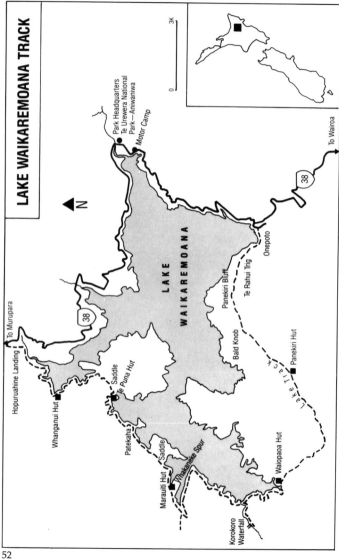

LAKE WAIKAREMOANA TRACK

N

LAKE WAIKAREMOANA

To Murupara

To Wairoa

38

38

Hopuruahine Landing

Whanganui Hut

Saddle
Te Puna Hut

Patekaha

Marauiti Hut

Saddle

Whakaneke Spur

Korokoro Waterfall

Waiopaoa Hut

Panekiri Hut

Lake Track

Bald Knob

Panekiri Bluff

Te Rahui Trig

Onepoto

Park Headquarters
Te Urewera National
Park—Aniwaniwa
Motor Camp

3K

0

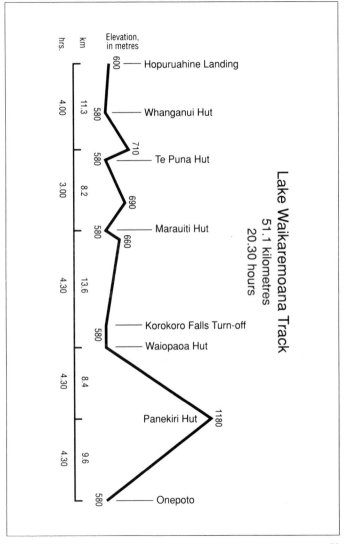

Elevation, in metres

Lake Waikaremoana Track
51.1 kilometres
20.30 hours

600 — Hopuruahine Landing

4.00 | 11.3

580 — Whanganui Hut

710

580 — Te Puna Hut

3.00 | 8.2

690

580 — Marauiti Hut

660

4.30 | 13.6

580 — Korokoro Falls Turn-off
580 — Waiopaoa Hut

4.30 | 8.4

Panekiri Hut — 1180

4.30 | 9.6

580 — Onepoto

hrs. km

53

HOPURUAHINE LANDING (600m) to TE PUNA HUT (580m)
via WHANGANUI HUT (580m)
and TE PUNA SADDLE (710m)
4.00 hours, 11.3km

Elevation:	Almost level; parts moderate
Terrain:	Bush; riparian

From SH 38, drive about 30 minutes by car north of the Aniwaniwa Visitor Centre to Hopuruahine Landing. If the river is low, walk 1 kilometre on the gravel access road down to the Hopuruahine River and the grassy camping area, where you can ford the river at the signpost. This cuts about 30 minutes off your tramp. If the river is high, the true track begins at the concrete bridge on SH 38, about 5 minutes further on by car. Following the true right of the river, the steep track passes through bush and joins the true track at the river. You first pass through some grassy flats bordering an inlet to the lake and then cross in bush over a small point to the Whanganui Hut (sleeps 18/stove) located between two streams which flow together behind the hut. Located only 5.7 kilometres from the northern road end, the hut is lightly used but convenient if you are travelling in the opposite direction and plan to catch an early morning bus.

Continuing on down from the Whanganui Stream, the track follows the shore of the lake for one hour to Tapuaenui Bay. Heading inland, the tramper faces a 100 metre 1 hour climb over a saddle emerging from the bush at Te Puna Hut (sleeps 18/stove) in a clearing by the lake.

TE PUNA HUT (580m) to MARAUITI HUT (580m)
via TE KOPUA SADDLE (690m)
3.00 hours, 8.2km

Elevation:	Almost level, parts moderate
Terrain:	Bush, riparian

This easy section of the track follows the lake shore by Upokororo and Tureia Bay opposite Patekaha Island. If the water level is low, you may avoid the 50-metre climb and cut across the grassy flats to the track on the other side. Next, traverse the peninsula to Te Totara Bay. With its lovely white sandy beaches Te Kopua Bay is a fine spot for camping. Then, for 90 metres, the track ascends a small saddle away from the lake and drops down to a swingbridge to the Marauiti Hut (sleeps 18/stove). From the swingbridge, trout are visible; unsurprisingly, this is a popular spot with anglers.

MARAUITI HUT (580m) toWAIOPAOA HUT (580m)
via WHAKANEKE SPUR (660m)
4.30 hours, 13.6km

Elevation: Almost level; parts moderate
Terrain: Bush, riparian
Special Features: Waterfall

From the hut you cross the Whakaneke Spur and drop down to the lake again cutting through Maori land on the edge of the Maraunui Inlet. You will pass a ranger station manned during the busy December-January season and, to your surprise, a cabin complete with TV antennae! The track continues around the edge of the lake rising and dropping as it passes a series of sheltered bays.

You will come next to a turn off to Korokoro Falls (45-60 minutes return). This bush-clad wide waterfall, one of the loveliest in the park, drops 22 metres off a rock face. The path to the waterfall winds through the bush and crosses a stream on some mossy rocks with a wire rope for balance.

It's only 45 minutes and $2^{1}/_{2}$ kilometres more to the hut on flat track, and a welcome break from the roots and tangles, up and downs, you've been managing up to now. The recently upgraded Waiopaoa Hut (sleeps 21/stove) sits away from the lake but a 5 minute stroll leads you to a fine beach. Numerous secluded camping spots lie between the beach and the hut.

WAIOPAOA HUT (580m) to PANEKIRI HUT (1180m)
4.30 hours, 8.4km

Elevation:	Steep; parts extremely steep
Terrain:	Bush
Special Features:	Lake views

This day requires the only significant climb of the track, and you may subtract 1 hour from the time allowed if instead you are travelling downhill from Panekiri to Waiopaoa. You will want to carry water for the trip. Beginning directly behind the hut, the track at first ascends gradually in bush, but steepens after about 2 kilometres. This steepness increases, gaining 250 metres in 1 kilometre, and at times you must grab onto roots and trees to pull yourself up. About half-way up, the track leaves the bush for a short time giving way to your first panoramic views of the lake, and a well deserved rest on the rocks. Twenty minutes later, you come to the base of huge rock outcrop with a small amount water trickling from its tops. Above this, the climb becomes more gradual and joins the main ridge. An hour and a half more over small bluffs and in and out of gullies brings you to the modern Panekiri Hut (sleeps 36/stove). The architecturally designed hut was enlarged in 1991 adding a dining and cooking area. The views are spectacular in all directions: north over the entire lake, and south to Napier and Hawke Bay. Watch out for the steep cliffs when you leave the hut; it's a good 500 metres down off the Panekiri Bluffs.

PANEKIRI HUT (1180m) to ONEPOTO (580m)
4.30 hours, 9.6km

Elevation:	Steep
Terrain:	Bush
Special Features:	Lake views

Since there is no water source from the hut to Onepoto, you'll want to carry some for the day. From the hut go directly into the bush and in 5 minutes you pass close to a bluff where there is a staircase and a 10 metre descent with a fixed rope for support. You wind up and down through mixed beech forest for 3 kilometres. Though the general trend of the walk is down, there are a few short rises and occasional breaks from the bush to view the lake or bluffs. After 1 hour you pass Bald Knob, a good place to rest. Undulating along the ridge for another hour and a half, you'll find Te Rahui Trig another restful spot to take in the last look of the lake. Look back to get a fine view of the cliffs. From here the track widens, the bush thins out, and you drop steadily to Onepoto where there is a day shelter and a boat ramp. From here, it's only a 5 minute walk to SH 38 where the sounds of civilization may jar you from the quiet contemplative mood you've enjoyed in the New Zealand bush.

ADDITIONAL INFORMATION

Huts may be full between October and March, so be sure to carry a tent. Hunters and fisherman frequent the bush any time of year, though less so in summer, and may share the huts. Wasps, at their height in March, have been a problem around some of the huts. In an attempt to control them, a yearly spraying programme has begun.

CONTACTS

Department of Conservation, Te Urewera National Park, Aniwaniwa Visitor Centre, Private Bag 2213, Wairoa		0-6-837 3803
City Connection, Wairoa		0-6-838 8533
Track transport (within park)	Bus	0-6-837 3836
	Boat	0-6-837 3729
Waikaremoana Motor Camp, Lake Waikaremoana		0-6-837 3826
Visitor Information (*i*), Marine Parade, Napier		0-6-835 7182
Visitor Information (*i*), 67 Fenton Street, Rotorua		0-7-348 5179

CHAPTER 8: **NORTH ISLAND, CENTRAL: TONGARIRO NATIONAL PARK**

ROUND MT NGAURUHOE TRACK

Tongariro still smokes...
The ancestral fires still burn
And the land lives on for all.

Te Heu Heu Tukino, 1887

In the heart of the North Island lies Tongariro, New Zealand's most heavily visited National Park. The three volcanoes, Mts Tongariro, Ngauruhoe, and Ruapehu, often still smoking, provide year-round recreation for many different outdoor enthusiasts. In summer, trampers scramble up the same peaks that, in the winter, skiers glide down. Others enjoy its peaceful walking tracks, a golf course, and snow lodges. One of the country's loveliest and best-known hotels, the Chateau, is located here next to the Visitor Centre.

The three volcanoes dominate the park. Mt Ruapehu (2796m), with its ski field, is the highest mountain on the North Island. At the summit crater, a sulphurous lake continues to steam; the last major eruption occurred in 1975. Mt Ngauruhoe (2291m), with its perfectly symmetrical cone, has continued to smoulder since its last eruption in 1975. Interestingly, Mt Tongariro, the lowest of the three (1968m), gave the park its namesake, because of it's focus in Maori legend and importance to the Maori people.

The park now comprises 75,500 hectares of barren tussock covered landscape with vegetation severely affected by recent eruptions. The park's extraordinary diversity makes for magnificent tramping. So wondrous a place can only be fully appreciated by those who venture into its depths. Through the penetrating quiet, disturbed only by a whisper of the wind, the tramper soon discovers the park's hidden magnificence in its barren slopes, emerald green pools, and steaming craters.

WEATHER

Park weather tends to change rapidly, and rain and high winds can strike without warning. Heavy snows accompanied by severe temperatures may occur anytime of year. All tracks in the park are exposed to these serious weather conditions, and trampers should be equipped for cold. An extra day or two is handy should it be necessary to wait out the bad weather.

Weather comes from the west, dropping large amounts of precipitation, up to 2500 millimetres per year, on this side of the mountain. The eastern side, the Rangipo Desert, boasts a barren dry landscape devoid of vegetation, with stark beauty found nowhere else in New Zealand.

BASE

The park is 341 kilometres from Auckland, 354 kilometres from Wellington, and 48 kilometres from Turangi. Access roads towards the Park's centre at Whakapapa Village exist on all sides, and it is a convenient destination from all areas of the North Island. State Highway 1 (the Desert Road) runs up the eastern side of the Park, and SH 4 provides access from the west. These are connected by SH 47 and 47 A to the north and west, and SH 49 to the southwest.

The centre of activity is the tiny village of Whakapapa on the slopes of Mt Ruapehu. At this starting point for most tramping in the park, there is a small store, garage, post office, hotel, motel, and motor camp, with cabins and tent sites. There are no banking facilities in the village. During high season, bookings, especially at the motor camp, are advised. Outside the Park in Ohakune, National Park, Turangi, and Waiouru you will find many more hotels, motels, camping, and backpacker's lodges.

Convenient bus and train services from Auckland and Wellington serves National Park and Ohakune. Connections from National Park to Whakapapa Village are available by minibus service provided by the Ski Haus. Check at the Visitor Centre for the latest information on transport into the park. Air New Zealand Link serves Taupo from Auckland and Wellington.

HISTORY

Maori history has always been prominent in the history of Mt Tongariro. Many early chiefs were buried on its slopes, and the land became tapu, or sacred. Thus this tradition prohibited man from entering; if he did, it was felt the mountain spirits would destroy him. The Maori thus sought to prevent anyone from climbing its slopes. They would often travel no further than part way up the mountain, often to Ketetahi Hot Springs.

Europeans were discouraged from travelling in the area until 1839, when John Bidwell became the first European to climb Mt Ngauruhoe. Without permission from the Maori owners, Mt Ruapehu was climbed by Sir George Grey in 1851. By the 1880s a steady stream of European explorers and geologists descended on the area. Ownership of the area of land which now comprises the National Park was disputed by several Maori tribes. In 1887, to prevent division of the sacred lands, the Maori Chief Te Heu Heu Tukino gave most of the three mountains to the government: "They shall be a sacred place of the Crown and a gift forever from me and my people." The gift laid the foundation for the national park system in New Zealand, and the area became the country's first National Park in 1894.

Railway service opened up to the area in 1908, and soon a road into the village at Whakapapa was cut, and its hotel, the Chateau, opened in 1929. Skifields were later developed in several areas of the park, further establishing Tongariro as one of New Zealand's main recreational centres.

TRACK ACCESS

The Round Mt Ngauruhoe Track is most conveniently begun from Whakapapa Village. One day can be cut off the trip by joining the track at Mangatepopo Hut, 15 minutes walk from the end of the Mangatepopo Road, which branches off SH 47 12 kilometres north of National Park. Starting from the eastern side of the park, the track may be accessed via a three-hour 700-metre ascent from the car park below Ketetahi Hot Springs, off SH 47A. You may join the track as well from the Desert Road (SH 1), where an hour and a half walk on a well-poled track leads you to the New Waihohonu Hut.

Trampers and Mt Ruapehu, Round Mt Ngauruhoe Track

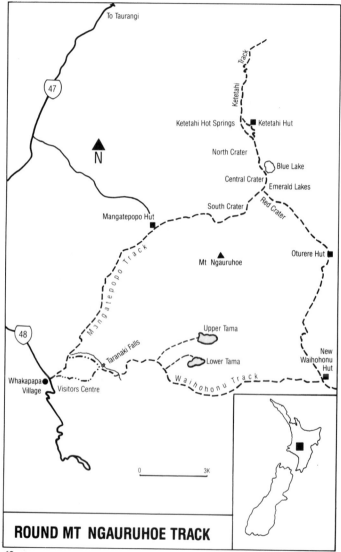

To Taurangi

47

North Crater

Ketetahi Hot Springs • Ketetahi Hut

Ketetahi Track

Blue Lake

Central Crater

Emerald Lakes

South Crater

Red Crater

Mangatepopo Hut

Mangatepopo Track

Mt Ngauruhoe

Oturere Hut

Upper Tama

Taranaki Falls

Lower Tama

48

New
Waihohonu
Hut

Waihohonu Track

Whakapapa
Village

Visitors Centre

0   3K

ROUND MT NGAURUHOE TRACK

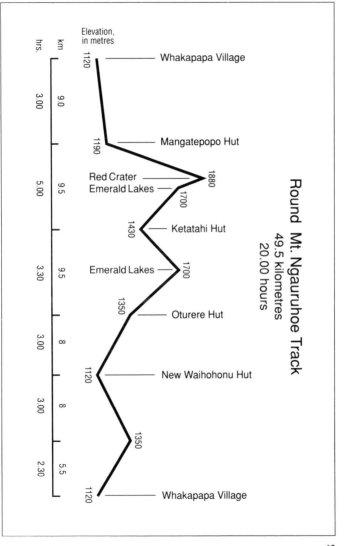

Elevation, in metres

hrs. km

Whakapapa Village — 1120

3.00 | 9.0

1190 — Mangatepopo Hut

5.00 | 9.5

Red Crater — 1880
Emerald Lakes — 1700

Ketatahi Hut — 1430

3.30 | 9.5

Emerald Lakes — 1700

1350 — Oturere Hut

3.00 | 8

1120 — New Waihohonu Hut

3.00 | 8

1350

2.30 | 5.5

1120 — Whakapapa Village

Round Mt. Ngauruhoe Track
49.5 kilometres
20.00 hours

THE TRACK

This three to four-day 49.5 kilometre moderate track encircles Mt Ngauruhoe on a well-poled or cairned route. The Tongariro Crossing between Mangatepopo Hut and the Ketetahi car park, a day hike option, passes through its most spectacular section. The complete circuit leaves the tramper with a better feel of the land's power and desolate beauty and permits him time to absorb more of the country's splendor.

WHAKAPAPA VILLAGE (1120m) to MANGATEPOPO HUT (1190m)
3.00 hours, 9km

Elevation:	Rolling
Terrain:	Scrub
Special Features:	Mountain views

Take the short road behind the Chateau, Ngauruhoe Place, to the turn off to the Lower Taranaki Falls. At first you pass through open grassland, and then enter thick bush with mountain beech and umbrella ferns. After 1 kilometre, take the trail's left branch across the footbridge that crosses Wairere Stream. Shortly the track leaves the bush, and undulates up and down for about 2½ hours before reaching Mangatepopo Hut (sleeps 24 / gas heater / summer warden). Serious erosion mars much of the track, which needs lots of work. Sweeping mountain views break some of the monotony. The hut affords good views of the next day's climb to the South Crater.

MANGATEPOPO HUT (1190m) to KETETAHI HUT (1430m) via RED CRATER (HIGH POINT)(1880m)
5.00 hours, 9.5km

Elevation:	Extremely steep; parts moderate, parts gradual
Terrain:	Scrub, rock
Special Features:	Mountain views, hot pools, volcanic craters

Tramper approaches launch, Abel Tasman Coast Track

Angelus Hut, Travers-Sabine Loop via Mt Robert

Travers Saddle Hut, Travers-Sabine Loop via Mt Robert

Douglas Rock Hut, Copland Track

Trampers approach Mangatepopo Hut, Round Mt Ngauruhoe Track

Some consider the Tongariro Crossing the finest one-day walk in New Zealand. Certainly the scenery is both unusual and spectacular. Warm clothing should be carried. The winds atop the craters can be icy cold, and there is little protection from rain or snow. On fine days, sun block, sunglasses and a sun hat are especially essential. Water should be carried since there is no potable water on route.

From the hut, follow the Mangatepopo Stream for the gradual ascent to Soda Springs, 5 minutes off the trail. As you approach, you can easily identify the springs by the sulphur smell. You then climb an extremely steep slope for 45 minutes to the base of Mt Ngauruhoe, and the saddle between Tongariro and Ngauruhoe. Here there is a sign pointing the way to the summit of Mt Ngauruhoe (3-4 hours return). This is a nice climb on a fine day, but beware of clouds and freezing rain which can come in quickly. Take care not to kick loose rocks on those walking below.

Follow the poled route along the moon-like flat South Crater until the track, straddling the South and Oturere Craters, heads north up a narrow ridge. You ascend to the day's high point above the steaming Red Crater, aptly named for the colour of its sheer

65

sides. From here a side trip to the summit of Tongariro will take an hour. Take the slippery loose trail down to the green Emerald Lakes, a good somewhat sheltered lunch spot. Take the left turn here for Ketetahi Hut, and backtrack to the junction the following day, although if time is short you may wish to turn right to Oturere Hut.

From Emerald Lakes cross Central Crater and in 1 kilometre climb 25 metres to crystal clear Blue Lake, passing above North Crater. Take a last look at Ngauruhoe and the edge of Red Crater, a fantastic scene. Begin the moderate switch-backed 300-metre descent on nicely graded trail to the popular though somewhat cramped Ketetahi Hut (sleeps 24/gas heater/summer warden) from where there are excellent views to Lakes Taupo and Rotoaira from the front door.

From the hut, the 30-minute side trip to the springs could while away your afternoon. The hot springs are known to the Maori for their health giving properties. From the hut you can see the steam from the springs, and you can bathe in one of the many shallow boulder-strewn pools.

KETETAHI HUT (1430m) to OTURERE HUT (1350m) via EMERALD LAKES (1700m) 3.30 hours, 9.5km

Elevation:	Parts steep, parts gradual
Terrain:	Scrub, rock
Special Features:	Mountain views, volcanic craters

Retrace your steps to Emerald Lakes, which will take 1^1/$_2$ to 2 hours. Descend the steep slope past Emerald Lakes through old lava flows to the flat, open Oturere Crater. You pass huge lava formations up to 10 metres high while enjoying fine views of Mt Ruapehu and Ngauruhoe. The poled route follows across the moonscape terrain to the large Oturere Hut (sleeps 30/gas heater), which is used somewhat less than other huts on this route. It provides a good low-level alternative route to the Tongariro Crossing if wishing to reach the Visitor Centre in poor weather.

OTURERE HUT(1350m) to NEW WAIHOHONU HUT (1120m)
3.00 hours, 8km

Elevation:	Gradual, parts steep
Terrain:	Scrub
Special Features:	Mountain views

This pleasant walk leaves the large volcanic formations behind, and although little total elevation is lost, for the first part of this section you cross up and down over several steep creek beds. About $1^1/_2$ kilometres before the hut, you cross a footbridge over Ohinepango Stream and ascend 80 metres through bush to the top of a knoll. Twenty minutes after beginning your descent, you emerge from the bush and arrive at the New Waihohonu Hut (sleeps 30/gas heater/summer warden). Worthwhile side trips include a visit to the historic Waihohonu Hut, built in 1901 (30 minutes return), and the crystal clear bubbling Ohinepango Springs (45 minutes return).

NEW WAIHOHONU HUT (1120m) to WHAKAPAPA VILLAGE (1120m) via TAMA SADDLE (1350m)
5.30 hours, 13.5km

Elevation:	Rolling
Terrain:	Scrub
Special Features:	Mountain views, volcanic formations

From the hut, follow the poled route between Mt Ruapehu and Ngauruhoe across the tussock fields 8 kilometres to the turn-off to Tama Lakes ($1^1/_2$ hours return to Upper Tama, 20 minutes to Lower Tama). The track undulates, crossing many small streams and gullies eroded by frost and rain before reaching its high point at Tama Saddle, just before the turn-off.

In about 2 hours more, you come to the junction of the Taranaki Falls Track. The right turn takes you to below the Falls to a pleasant lunch spot, and continues on to Cascade Falls and the turn-off to

Mt Ruapeheu, Round Mt Ngauruhoe Track

Mangatepopo Hut. The upper track, a well cared for gravel path, shows more signs of civilization as it winds through open country, with obvious pumice and ash layers from previous eruptions, and good views of Mt Ruapehu. Both tracks finish near the THC Chateau.

CAMPING

If a hut is crowded you may camp in the vicinity and use the facilities, such as toilets, gas, etc. A charge of one hut ticket per person per night is made in this instance. Normally, however, camping is prohibited within 800 metres of a hut, and 200 metres of any track or road in the park.

CONTACTS

Department of Conservation, Tongariro National Park, Whakapapa
Visitors Centre, Mt Ruapehu   0-7-892 3729
Whakapapa Holiday Park, Whakapapa Village, Mt Ruapehu

                                                  0-7-892 3897
Alpine Scenic Tours, Turangi   0-7-378 6305
Ski Haus, Carroll Street, National Park   0-7-892 2854
Visitor Information *(i)*, 13 Tongariro Street, Taupo 0-7-378 9000
Visitor Information *(i)*, Ngawaka Place, Turangi   0-7-386 8999

CHAPTER 9: **NORTH ISLAND, WEST: EGMONT NATIONAL PARK**

ROUND-THE-MOUNTAIN TRACK

The body roams the mountains; and the spirit is set free.
                                                    Hsu Hsia-k'o

At the centre of Mount Egmont National Park, Mt Egmont/Taranaki
(2518m) dominates the skyline from all nearby view points, and
moulds the character of the area. Its symmetrical cone, one of the
most beautiful sights in all of New Zealand, and often compared
with Japan's Mt Fujiyama, casts a spell over the surrounding plains.
On a fine day, Egmont/Taranaki can be seen from as far away as the
northern part of the South Island. Yet, on one of those frequent
cloudy or foggy days, the mountain may go unnoticed by visitors
unaware of its existence. Exerting a spiritual grace on all who pass
near, the mountain, enveloped in mist and shrouded in snow,
captures all who are blessed with the opportunity to walk in its
shadow.

   The ever-present isolated dormant volcano last erupted in 1755,
more than two centuries ago. Over the previous centuries devastating
eruptions have moulded its terrain, creating rivers, forest and fertile
lowlands. Unlike the volcanoes of Tongariro National Park, Mt
Egmont/Taranaki rises out of lush green pastures, its upper reaches
covered with snow above the treeline for all but the summer
months.

   The Round-the-Mountain Track (RMT) circles this lovely
mountain at elevations between 500 and 1500 metres. The 320
kilometres of tracks interlace amid a network of nine park huts and
three mountain club huts. Three major access roads, climbing to a
level of 900 metres, allow the visitor to approach the bushline of the
mountain, or on a fine day to hike to any of its higher points. Because
of its easy accessibility, the climb to the top of Mt Egmont/Taranaki

is one of the most popular in New Zealand. Trampers hiking to the top should be equipped with food, warm clothing and water, and leave a note of their intention at the Visitor Centre. They must pay close attention to the weather, and if clouds move in, abort the climb. Clouds may take only a few hours to envelope the mountain. If climbing the mountain's eastern slope from North Egmont, bad weather coming from the west may not be noticed until late in the day.

WEATHER

The weather here is typical of any mountainous area of New Zealand. Large amounts of rain, high winds, and plunging temperatures are possible even in summer. Westerlies blowing in from the Tasman Sea drop more rainfall on the park's western side. Snow falls freely during the winter, with a snow level as low as 1000 metres common. The average rainfall at 1000 metres is 6500 millimetres per year, and at 2000 metres is an astounding 8000 millimetres per year. The driest periods occur in January and February. Radial patterns of streams have carved out the mountain slopes at all angles from the summit and created deep gullies and streams on all sides of the mountain. Crossing in and out of these gullies, up and over tangled tree roots, over bridges and aluminum ladders, is the experience of the tramper on the Round-the-Mountain Track.

BASE

New Plymouth (population 45,000) on the North Island's western shore is 164 kilometres NW of Wanganui at the junction of SH 3 and 45. The city lies on the edge of a large peninsula that juts out into the Tasman Sea. The peninsula itself is dominated by the cone of Taranaki. The economy once centred around the lush farmlands, but the area has now developed its own industry. Oil wells, both on and off shore, have been tapped, and some operate a stone's throw from the city centre.

The bustling community has numerous places to stay, from backpacker's lodges to motels and hotels, with plenty of stores for resupply. Besides the huts on the mountain, there is backpacker's accommodation at the Camphouse at North Egmont, and at Konini Lodge at Dawson Falls. Stratford Mountain House at East Egmont and Dawson Falls Tourist Lodge offer more luxurious accommodation.

Transport to New Plymouth is easy. InterCity and Newmans buses run daily from Auckland, Hamilton and Wellington. White Star bus services New Plymouth from Wellington. Air New Zealand Link flies to New Plymouth several times a day from Auckland and Wellington.

HISTORY

According to Maori legend, Taranaki once stood far to the east, in Tongariro National Park. The mountains there fought for the love of beautiful volcano Pihanga. Taranaki, defeated by Tongariro, fled west at night, carving the path of the Wanganui River. He fell asleep, and upon waking at dawn, found himself trapped in the far west by a spur of the Pouakai Range. The Maori believe that when the mountain becomes shrouded in mist, it means Taranaki is weeping for his lost love.

It may be that Abel Tasman, the European discoverer of New Zealand, missed seeing the mountain. His 1642 logs, when he was known to be in the area, contain no record of its sighting. The mountain's original name was Taranaki or "barren mountain" as the Maori knew it. James Cook, sailing up the coast, renamed the mountain Egmont after his chief patron, the Earl of Egmont. The Maori stuck by its original name, and today the peak shares both names.

The first English settler to reach the top of Mt Egmont was Ernst Dieffenbach in 1839. Fanthams Peak, the mountain's secondary cone, bears the name of the first woman European climber Fanny Fantham, who scaled the peak in 1887. As more English began to arrive, they clashed with local Maori tribes over possession of land. In the 1890s, however, a track was cut to Holly Flat, and Mt Egmont became a popular spot for vacationers. In 1885 Thomas Dawson discovered the falls which now bear his name. The area was fully surveyed in 1901, after which full-scale development of tracks, roads and huts began. In July 1881, a symmetrical area in a radius of 9.5 kilometres from the summit was protected, and in 1900 the area was set aside as a national park, the second in New Zealand. Subsequent additions of small sections of land to the National Park have broken the symmetry.

TRACK ACCESS

There are three main approaches to Mt Egmont. From Highway 3, between Stratford and New Plymouth, the Egmont Road departs 13 kilometres from New Plymouth, and ascends the mountain another 16 kilometres to North Egmont (957m). From Stratford, Pembroke Road goes 15 kilometres to Stratford Mountain House, and 3 kilometres more to Stratford Plateau (1140m). Dawson Falls (900m) is on the Manaia Road approximately 23 kilometres from Stratford. A private car is the easiest form of transport to the track, since you can drive to one of the three access points, circle the mountain, and return to your car.

There is no public transport to any of the higher levels of the mountain. Mountain Excursions, a transport service, runs daily from New Plymouth to the North Egmont Visitor Centre and back. Contact the Visitor Centre for further information.

THE TRACK

This strenuous high-level 39.8 kilometre track can be walked in either direction in three to four days. The tramper should be fit, able to handle muddy, slippery tracks, and patient with the many up and downs of the continually undulating track. If you start from the North Egmont Visitor Centre, remember that you need an additional hour for the 563 metre ascent up either "The Puffer" or "The Razorback" to join the RMT. Since huts are a bit more evenly spaced walking clockwise, the track description follows this direction starting from Stratford Plateau. There is direct access to the RMT from either Stratford Plateau or Dawson Falls. The high-level (alpine) variation is described first.

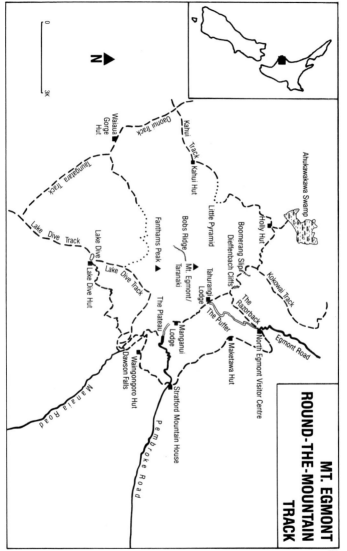

MT. EGMONT ROUND-THE-MOUNTAIN TRACK

73

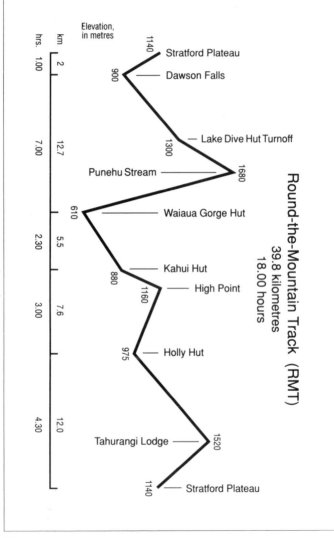

Round-the-Mountain Track (RMT)
39.8 kilometres
18.00 hours

Elevation, in metres

hrs. | km

1140 — Stratford Plateau
900 — Dawson Falls
1300 — Lake Dive Hut Turnoff
1680
Punehu Stream —
610 — Waiaua Gorge Hut
880 — Kahui Hut
1160 — High Point
975 — Holly Hut
1520
Tahurangi Lodge —
1140 — Stratford Plateau

1.00 — 2
7.00 — 12.7
2.30 — 5.5
3.00 — 7.6
4.30 — 12.0

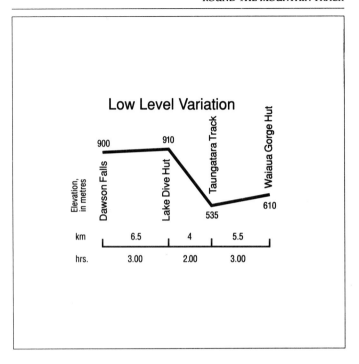

Low Level Variation

900	910			
Dawson Falls	Lake Dive Hut	Taungatara Track	Waiaua Gorge Hut	
			610	
		535		

Elevation, in metres

km	6.5	4	5.5
hrs.	3.00	2.00	3.00

STRATFORD PLATEAU (1140m) to DAWSON FALLS (900m)
1 hour, 2km

Elevation:	Moderate
Terrain:	Bush, riparian
Special Features:	Mountain views

From the flat car park at the Stratford Plateau, 3 kilometres above East Egmont and the Stratford Mountain House, you begin to descend immediately on a well-formed tourist track with wooden steps through thick bush. Soon you drop into the "goblin" forest where moss hangs from the trees above you. A side-trip to Wilkies Pool is worthwhile, and upon returning to the signed track you'll

75

visit Twin Falls, Bubbling Springs, and Victoria Falls. In about 1 hour from your departure, you'll come to Dawson Falls, with the Visitor Centre and its lovely park displays, Dawson Falls Tourist Lodge, and Konini Lodge, backpacker's accommodation. You may register your intentions here if you failed to do so at the Pembroke Road Field Centre on the road into the Park.

DAWSON FALLS (900m) to WAIAUA GORGE HUT (610m)
via HIGH POINT at PUNEHU STREAM (1680m)
(HIGH LEVEL ALPINE ROUTE)
7 hours, 12.7km

Elevation:	Parts extremely steep, parts gradual
Terrain:	Grassland, riparian, rock
Special Features:	Mountain views, waterfall

From here you can choose either the high-level route to Waiaua Gorge or the low-level route to Lake Dive and on to Waiaua Gorge. The latter route takes a day longer than the former. In fine summer weather, the high level RMT with its superb views and alpine scenery should be your choice. The route should not, however, be attempted in winter or in poor weather. The high-level (alpine) section from Dawson Falls to Waiaua Gorge Hut is described below.

Continuing to Waiaua Gorge on the high-level route, follow the signs to the Summit Track. Climb up now for 20 minutes passing through the "goblin" forest to the infamous Egmont Steps. These steps are spaced far apart and are intended less to aid the climber than to prevent erosion. In 30 minutes, you pass Hillarys seat, honouring the New Zealand climber's first ascent of Mt Everest in 1953. Fifteen minutes more brings you to the welcome Hooker Shelter (1140m). After this, the track becomes steeper and more eroded. In 1^1/$_2$hours you reach the turnoff to the NZ Alpine Club Lodge, Kapuni Lodge (1400m). In 10 more minutes you begin the poled traverse over tussock and scrub across Fanthams Peak, then 30 minutes later you reach the turn-off to Lake Dive Hut. If you wish to continue onto Waiaua Gorge Hut, turn right and continue upwards, cutting one day off the RMT, a total of 7 hours from Dawson Falls. Or, if you wish to descend to Lake Dive, turn left at the junction and begin your 30 minute descent to the hut, this time down more seemingly innumerable steps and short ladders as you lose elevation quickly to meet Lake Dive Hut.

Continuing on the high-level route after your right turn, you slowly gain more elevation as you sidle around the alpine slopes of Taranaki. The slopes of the Punehu Gorge, at 1680 metres, mark the high point for the day. It is 1¹/₂ hours from the turn-off until you drop to the Mangahume Hut site. The hut, now removed, is still on older maps. Continue to follow the poles, but you will find that years of traffic has eroded a narrow track which can be followed even during periods of low visibility. The route then wriggles through some rocky outcrops, where hands are required, and the rock is loose. In another 30 minutes you sidle around Bobs Ridge with its cliffs towering above you. Finally, as you enter the scrub, you lose elevation quickly on a muddy and rutted track that enters the forest in 30 more minutes. Negotiating this slippery section takes good balance and careful attention to the track. One hour total of descent brings you to the Brames Falls viewpoint, as you enter thick bush above the Waiaua Gorge. From the viewpoint, the waterfall can be seen up the gorge tumbling into the bush-clad creek below. At the junction of the Taungatara Track (RMT low-level) take a right turn. You will soon be climbing steeply over roots down into the Waiaua River, highlighted by a climb up an aluminum ladder on the steep opposite side to reach the Waiaua Gorge Hut (sleeps 20/stove). From the edge of the gorge, a stone's throw from the front porch, you'll enjoy fine views of the peak and gorge itself.

DAWSON FALLS (900m) to LAKE DIVE HUT (910m)
(LOW LEVEL ROUTE)
3 hours, 6.5km

Elevation: Rolling; parts extremely steep
Terrain: Bush

From Dawson Falls Visitor Centre, take the Hasties Hill track through thick bush. This all weather section of the RMT was opened in 1986. Most of the route takes you through bush, up and down creek beds, ladders and stairs, with limited views. The high point crosses a bog on a boardwalk providing good views to lava flows from Fanthams Peak. In 3 hours, you'll be happy to reach Lake Dive Hut (sleeps 16/stove) and the "Beehive", stacks of lava formations dating from several thousand years ago.

LAKE DIVE HUT (910m) to WAIAUA GORGE HUT (610m) via TAUNGATARA TRACK (535m) (LOW LEVEL TRACK) 5 hours, 9.5km

Elevation: Parts moderate, parts extremely steep
Terrain: Bush

The low-level track from Lake Dive Hut to Waiaua Gorge Hut constitutes one of the most difficult and longest stretches of the track. Although there is little total elevation change, you climb in and out of gulches and creek-beds amid mud and tangles of roots. The Taungatara (between Lake Dive and Waiaua) and Oaonui (between Waiaua and the Kahui Track) Tracks do not meet the standards of the rest of the RMT. Take care with some of the creek crossings in high water, especially at Punehu and Mangahume Streams.

WAIAUA GORGE HUT (610m) to HOLLY HUT (975m) via KAHUI HUT (880m) and HIGH POINT (1160m) 5.30 hours, 13.1km

Elevation: Gradual
Terrain: Bush, scrub
Special Features: Mountain views

The track starts out on the Oaonui (low-level) track and for 15 minutes is of good quality, first crossing a footbridge over a stream to join the access track at Oaonui Stream. After this point, it deteriorates, and in 1½ hours from the Gorge you, thankfully, reach the junction with the Kahui Track. This slippery muddy section, climbing in and out of creek beds, taxes even the most fit. Turning right at the Kahui Track, the track improves as you climb uphill gradually 1 hour and 270 metres to the old Kahui Hut (sleeps 6). There are grand views out to the west and towards the mountain crater. A bit less than half-way in the day's journey, lunch or morning tea is the order of the day.

From the hut you climb again gradually around Kahui Hill to the Puniho Track. Then it ascends to the day's high point below Little Pyramid (1160m), following marker poles after crossing several stream beds. The view to the west continues to be impressive. As you wind through gorges and over creeks, the track then descends and winds around Upson and Peters Stream. A steep 70 metre climb from the stream brings you to large modern Holly Hut (sleeps 38/stove). There are good views and side-trips from here to Bells Falls, and the Ahukawakawa Swamp.

HOLLY HUT (975m) to STRATFORD PLATEAU (1140m) via TAHURANGI LODGE (1520m)
4.30 hours, 12km

Elevation:	Moderate
Terrain:	Scrub
Special Features:	Mountain views

Just past the junction with the Ahukawakawa Track, you climb steadily over some wooden steps for 1 hour until you reach the Kokowai Track. You can readily see back to the swamp and the Pouakai Range. This section is famous for the winds that blow between Pouakai and Egmont.

Now you pass into a high-level section of the RMT, which makes a steady ascent to Tahurangi Lodge and finally drops to the Stratford Plateau. From the junction of the RMT and the Kokowai Tracks, you cross in and out of gullies to Boomerang Slip. Cross the rocky active area quickly, and don't linger as rockfall is extremely dangerous. You have your first views from here of the North Egmont Complex. Sidle next around the Dieffenbach Cliffs, and if you started in North Egmont, begin your descent on the Razorback to the Visitor Centre. There are fine views back to the slopes of Taranaki. The most direct route to the Stratford Plateau turns right at the Razorback, and traverses above the NZ Alpine Club's Tahurangi Lodge and finally drops down to the car park, the point from where you began your journey several days ago.

CONTACTS

Department of Conservation, New Plymouth Field Centre,
    PO Box 462, 220 Devon St. West, New Plymouth 0-6-758 0433
Department of Conservation Field Centre, Pembroke Road,
    Stratford   0-6-765 5144
North Egmont Visitor Centre, Egmont Road, North Egmont
                                                 0-6-756 8710
Visitor Information *(i)*, 81 Liardet Street, New Plymouth
                                                 0-6-758 6086

CHAPTER 10: SOUTH ISLAND, NORTH: ABEL TASMAN NATIONAL PARK AND NORTH WEST NELSON STATE FOREST PARK

COAST TRACK/HEAPHY TRACK/ WANGAPEKA TRACK

*...and like a carpet at your feet, in endless gradations of
light and shade, the New Zealand bush spreads out in green
waves downwards to the edge of the ocean*
Andreas Reischek, 1884

The northwestern section of the South Island has been preserved into two parks: Abel Tasman National Park and North West Nelson State Forest Park. This area plays host to numerous travellers who come to hike three well-known tracks: The Coast Track in Abel Tasman National Park, and North West Nelson State Forest Park's Heaphy and Wangapeka Tracks. Characteristics of these parks include their glorious bush sections, sandy beaches and more sun than rain. The Coast Track and the Heaphy Track attract thousands of trampers each year who seek well-maintained and graded tracks. The Wangapeka Track by contrast appeals to those savouring isolation and more challenging terrain.

WEATHER

Abel Tasman National Park park is well known for its mild sunny climate. It can be hot (25°C) and a bit humid in the high summer months. Milder temperatures come in the autumn and winter. Poor unsettled weather presents much less of a threat on the Coast Track than on any other walking track in New Zealand.

North West Nelson State Forest Park supports a wetter climate, especially on the western side, and up to 2500 millimetres of rain per year falls in this area. Rivers and streams recently bridged make many, but not all, crossings easy. As a result of the high amounts of rainfall, rivers rise rapidly and can become dangerously high. Several high water routes are options on the Heaphy and Wangapeka Tracks. River crossings should not be attempted by inexperienced parties. Care should be exercised in rocky, steep or muddy areas because of wet, slippery footing.

BASE

If planning to walk any of the three tracks, Nelson, 135 kilometres west of Picton, is a convenient starting point. One of the most pleasant cities in New Zealand, baked in sunshine, Nelson (population: 43,000) is known for its orchards of apples and kiwifruit and its berry fields, and as one of the country's busiest ports. Over the last few years the area has become a center for craftsmen, especially potters. A large shopping district offers a wide variety of supplies.

In the past few years the amount of accommodation has increased markedly in Nelson but during the high summer it can be overcrowded. A lot of smaller private budget accommodation has sprung up due to the pressing need for more space. Backpacker's accommodation, motor camps, hostels, motels and hotels are all available.

Nelson is served by InterCity bus lines which connect to/from the Picton ferry to the North Island, and the train south to Christchurch. Daily bus services on InterCity connect as well to/from Westport, Greymouth and the Glaciers. Mount Cook Landline serves Nelson from Christchurch via Lewis Pass and via Picton and Blenheim. They also have service between Christchurch and Westport with connections to Karamea, on the western end of the Heaphy and Wangapeka Tracks. White Star bus lines serve Nelson from Christchurch, Greymouth and Westport.

Nelson's small but busy airport is served both by Ansett Airlines and Air New Zealand Link. There are several flights a day to

Christchurch and Auckland, and many across the Cook Strait to Wellington, your connecting point for most North Island destinations.

If just walking the Coast Track, Nelson is a good starting and return point. Trampers beginning the Wangapeka or Heaphy from the east, usually begin in Nelson or Motueka. If starting from the west both tracks end near Karamea, a small township 97 kilometres north of Westport on SH 67, located at the end of the road on the northern end on the South Island's West Coast. It can best be described as "off the beaten track". You'll find several backpacker's lodges, a motel, a hotel and town pub. It's a fine place to re-supply and rest if walking both the Wangapeka and Heaphy Tracks.

THE ABEL TASMAN COAST TRACK

Although a relatively small National Park, the Abel Tasman is one of New Zealand's most heavily visited. Here golden sand beaches lapped by crystal clear water stretch along the northern shores of the South Island. For the tramper, miles of brilliant coastline beg for exploration. Until recently, this area was relatively unknown, but in the last few years the number of visitors has exceeded 30,000 per year, although a large number of these are campers or day excursioners. Fortunately, the park has not yet been spoiled. However, the crowds bring many problems: noise, overcrowding at the huts, rubbish, and some difficulty with water pollution. It is up to all of us to work to preserve the sanctuary of this gorgeous coastline so that others may continue to enjoy it in years to come.

This is not the typical New Zealand tramp; there are no passes to cross, hills to climb or rivers to ford. The reasonably flat, wide, and well-marked track makes the 47 kilometre trip accessible to beginners and families, and merits a rating of easy. Many negotiate the entire track in trainers, as if on an afternoon stroll. If you can handle the crowds, it's well worth a visit. If not, try late autumn,

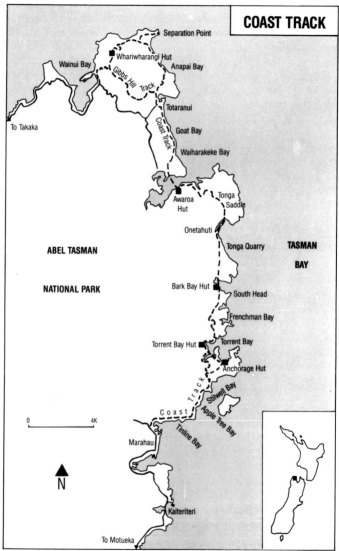

COAST TRACK

Separation Point

Whariwharangi Hut

Wainui Bay

Anapai Bay

Gibbs Hill Track

To Takaka

Totaranui

Coast Track

Goat Bay

Waiharakeke Bay

Awaroa Hut

Tonga Saddle

Onetahuti

ABEL TASMAN

Tonga Quarry

TASMAN

BAY

NATIONAL PARK

Bark Bay Hut

South Head

Frenchman Bay

Torrent Bay Hut

Torrent Bay

Anchorage Hut

0   4K

Stilwell Bay

Coast   Track

Apple Tree Bay

Marahau

Tinline Bay

N

Kaiteriteri

To Motueka

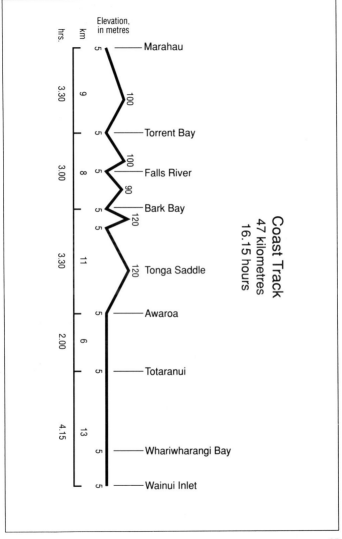

Coast Track
47 kilometres
16.15 hours

Elevation, in metres

hrs.	km		
	5		Marahau
3.30	9	100	
	5		Torrent Bay
3.00	8	100	Falls River
	5	90	
	5		Bark Bay
	5	120	
3.30	11	120	Tonga Saddle
	5		Awaroa
2.00	6		
	5		Totaranui
4.15	13		
	5		Whariwharangi Bay
	5		Wainui Inlet

winter or spring; bring your swimming suit and suntan lotion, settle back and relax, and enjoy several days meandering up the coastline.

An "Abel Tasman National Park Facilities Use Pass" must be purchased before departing on the track. It can be bought at Department of Conservation offices in Nelson, Motueka and Takaka Visitor Centres and even on the launch. Huts do not have gas rings and, especially in summer, are overcrowded, so a tent is recommended.

Be sure to study the tidetables since you can cross the Awaroa Inlet only two hours before or after low tide, and there is no alternative route.

HISTORY

The first European to sight New Zealand was the Dutch explorer Abel Tasman. In 1642 his ships spent their first night off the northern end of the park and the next day engaged with the Maori in combat. In 1827 the French explorer Dumont D'Urville first explored the park.

In the early 1850s William Gibbs built an elaborate settlement at Totaranui. Because of barren soil and sparse timber, attempts to farm the area remained modest. Shipbuilders settled the Awaroa area around this time, but the timber lasted only into the early 1900s. The region has never supported a year-round population. Those who come today are overseas visitors or New Zealanders on holiday. In 1942 the area became a national park.

TRACK ACCESS

Connections to the track have greatly improved in the recent years. Bus service from Nelson to Marahau and Totaranui and return is provided by Skyline Travel (summer only) and Abel Tasman National Park Enterprises (all year). A popular launch service, run by Abel Tasman National Park Enterprises departs daily from Kaiteriteri from late September to early June, stopping along the Coast Track (Tinline Bay, Torrent Bay, Bark Bay, Tonga Bay, Awaroa, Totaranui). The morning launch will drop trampers off at all stops and, starting back from Totaranui about noontime, will pick them up again. The launch also links up with bus connections to Nelson. Neither bus or launch services operate on Christmas Day. Several day cruise options are available as well: a cruise with bush walks, a cruise and fly option, and an evening launch.

If ending your tramp at Whariwharangi Hut you will have to back track to Totaranui to meet transportation, or walk to the Takaka-Totaranui Road and catch the bus.

MARAHAU (5m) to ANCHORAGE and/or TORRENT BAY (5m) via SADDLE (100m)
3.30 hours, 9km

Elevation:	Almost level
Terrain:	Coastline, scrub

From the Marahau car park, the track begins across the boardwalk, 1 kilometre from the information sign and the small restaurant. Cross over the Marahau estuary to the park boundary and logbook and follow the coastline for 30 minutes to Tinline Bay, the first stop for the launch service. In 500 metres you will pass the turn off to the Castle Rock - Inland Track. The track ambles along the coastline 20 metres or so above the water, passing Appletree and Stilwell Bays. From the side track to Stilwell Bay, you slowly gain elevation as you cross inland passing across some small ridges and a signed junction. A left turn will bring you to Torrent Bay in 1 hour, a right turn to the Anchorage Hut in 1 hour. A few years ago, a brush fire burnt out much of this next section, and you must cross a hot, dry, bushy stretch no matter which turn you choose. Anchorage Hut (sleeps 32/stove/camping/summer warden) is located in a grassy area behind a sweeping sandy beach. Camping can be found at Te Pukatea Bay and Torrent Bay. To reach Torrent Bay from Anchorage Hut, walk west up the beach, paying attention to the signs to the estuary. At low tide cross the mudflats and follow poles with orange discs (some with distinguishing footprint markers) north to the small public campground. If the tide is high, you can take the track around the west side of the bay to the Torrent Bay Hut (sleeps 8/

stove). Crossing the flats from Anchorage to Torrent Bay takes about 25 minutes; the track requires 45 minutes. Torrent Bay, a lovely setting, has a number of private homes. If you are a member of the guided tour, this will be your stop for three nights.

TORRENT BAY (5m) to BARK BAY (5m) VIA SADDLE (100m) and FALLS RIVER SWINGBRIDGE (5m) and SOUTH HEAD VIEWPOINT (90m)
3.00 hours, 8km

Elevation:	Rolling
Terrain:	Coastline, scrub

From the Torrent Bay settlement, follow the large orange discs along the beach. Next climb 100 metres up a small saddle and past Kilby Stream. You will get views of Frenchman Bay and may take a side trip to a good viewpoint (30 minutes return). Then you drop down to the Falls River (5m) and cross the suspension bridge. Next you climb up again past the side track to Sandfly Bay and the viewpoint to South Head (20 minutes return). Descend about 100 metres to the modern Bark Bay Hut (sleeps 28/stove). Fine camping is found along the spit between the estuary and the sea.

BARK BAY (5m) to AWAROA (5m) VIA SADDLE (120m)
3.30 hours and 11km

Elevation:	Rolling
Terrain:	Coastline, bush

The low-tide route from Bark Bay crosses the spit in about 10 minutes. The high tide route on the western side of the bay begins behind the hut and takes about 30 minutes. From the north side of the bay the track climbs 120 metres up over a spur and drops down into Tonga Quarry, an old granite quarry (about 1 hour). The track climbs 100 metres again above cliffs and drops to the glorious

Onetahuti Beach where there is camping and irresistible swimming. It's 1 kilometre across the long span of golden beach to the crossing of Richardson stream. Here the water can be very deep at high tide, especially for small children. The well-maintained track ascends 120 metres to Tonga Saddle and then drops again, passing near private property - an airstrip, a fruit stand, and summer homes, before you emerge via Venture Creek to the Awaroa estuary. A short jaunt around the bay's edge brings you to Awaroa Hut (sleeps 30/stove/camping). You should have carefully studied the tidetables since you can cross the Awaroa Inlet only 2 hours before or after low tide, and there is no alternative route.

AWAROA (5m) to TOTARANUI (5m)
2.00 hours, 6km

Elevation:	Rolling
Terrain:	Coastline, bush
Special Features:	Estuary crossing

As there is no all-tidal route across the inlet, follow the now familiar orange discs to Pound Creek (40 minutes). Climbing a low saddle, the track follows a small creek and comes to another lovely small beach at Waiharakeke Bay, where there is camping (1 hour). From the north end of the bay, the track rises a bit and then drops into Goat Bay (no camping) and next passes Skinner Point for a nice view of Totaranui. Another 15 minutes and you'll arrive at Totaranui, where there is a ranger station, restroom, and a large public camping area. In late December and January, it gets extremely crowded. Trampers on the track may stay at the campground for the night without a reservation for a minimal fee in addition to their "Usage Pass". From here, you may catch the return bus or launch to Marahau or Kaiteriteri. Trampers may also choose to walk further north towards Anapai Bay, away from the crowds.

TOTARANUI (5m) to WHARIWHARANGI HUT (5m)
3.00 hours, 9km

Elevation:	Rolling
Terrain:	Bush, coastline, scrub

From the Visitor Centre, continue up the coast, and after crossing the inlet, take the left fork, up a 100-metre saddle and follow the creek to Anapai Bay (40 minutes), where there is camping. Continue northward to Separation Cove, breaking out through the bush just below the lighthouse at Mutton Cove. On a clear day you can see as far back as Nelson, and for many the sweeping view of Farewell Spit will be the highlight of the trip. On winter days, seals frequent the rocks near the shore. When you have retraced your tracks back to the saddle, the road meanders through the scrub to an old farmhouse converted to a National Park Hut at Whariwharangi Bay (sleeps 14). If you wish to return to Totaranui, where transport is readily available, you must retrace your steps, or tackle the high and dry Gibbs Hill Track (405m). Or, if you've arranged for transport, you may walk 4 kilometres on the road to the car park at Wainui Inlet, or head out to the road to flag down the bus.

TIDES

Tidetables are posted in all huts. If the tide is high, use the all tidal routes at Bark Bay and Torrent Bay. The tables must be consulted to cross the Awaroa Inlet.

GUIDED TOURS

Abel Tasman National Park Enterprises offers a four day guided walk through the park with three nights at their lodge at Torrent Bay. The trip begins with a ride up the coastline on their launch. You disembark at Tonga Bay, and spend the day walking back to the lodge. The next two days you walk the tracks in the Torrent Bay area, basing yourself at the lodge, with its hot showers, home cooking, and dormitory-style bedrooms. If you prefer not to walk, you may spend the day along the lovely beach swimming, fishing or canoeing. The final day you walk the coastline to Marahau. All belongings are carried for you.

HEAPHY TRACK

North West Nelson's best known track, the Heaphy Track, a scenic traverse connects Golden Bay with the West Coast, draws up to 4000 trampers per year. Diversity of landscape, easy terrain and spectacular coastal scenery make it popular with both kiwis and overseas visitors.

HISTORY

Thought to be an important source for food, the legendary moa may have drawn Maori tribes into the area of the Heaphy River around the sixteenth century. Charles Heaphy, the first European to explore the area, hiked up the West Coast as far as the Heaphy River in 1846. Later while looking for gold, James Mackay and John Clark explored the eastern portion of the track to Collingwood. The Heaphy Track was surveyed by John Saxon in 1888, but both the Heaphy and Wangapeka Tracks fell into disrepair after the failure to find gold. The unique landscapes of the Heaphy track however still attracted scientists who set aside Gouland Downs as a scenic reserve in 1915.

After North West Nelson State Forest Park was established, the track was extensively upgraded in the 1970s. New huts were erected, direction signs placed, and boardwalks built across the excessively muddy areas. At this time there were serious thoughts about building a road from Collingwood to Karamea. Conservationists, concerned about the damage to the Downs and nikau palms, began a campaign to popularize the tramp and discourage builders. Today the plan seems forgotten, but ironically, it helped make the track one of the most popular in New Zealand.

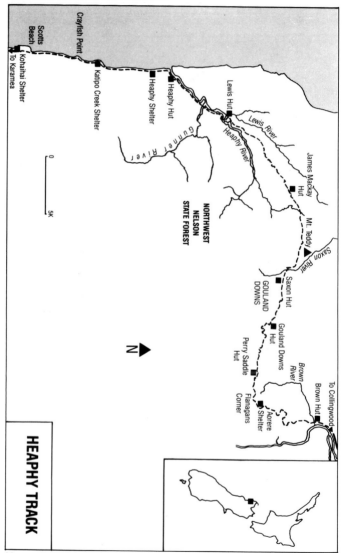

HEAPHY TRACK

Scotts Beach

Crayfish Point

Kohaihai Shelter
To Karamea

Katipo Creek Shelter

Heaphy Shelter

Heaphy Hut

Gunner River

Lewis Hut

Lewis River

Heaphy River

James Mackay Hut

Mt. Teddy

NORTHWEST
NELSON
STATE FOREST

Saxon River

Saxon Hut

GOULAND
DOWNS

Gouland Downs
Hut

Perry Saddle
Hut

Brown
River

Flanagans
Corner

Aorere
Shelter

Brown Hut

To Collingwood

0

5K

N

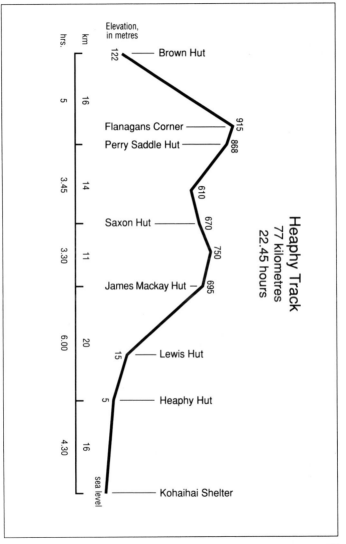

Heaphy Track
77 kilometres
22.45 hours

Elevation, in metres

hrs. km

Brown Hut — 122
5 — 16
Flanagans Corner — 915
Perry Saddle Hut — 868
3.45 — 14
610
Saxon Hut — 670
3.30 — 11
750
James Mackay Hut — 695
6.00 — 20
Lewis Hut — 15
Heaphy Hut — 5
4.30 — 16
Kohaihai Shelter — sea level

TRACK ACCESS

For the Heaphy Track, good transport is available from local operators who service both ends of the track. From Nelson, the Golden Bay Connection departs daily except Sunday to Collingwood, a tiny town on the island's northeastern shore. From here, Collingwood Bus Services will transport you the 35 kilometres to Brown Hut (sleeps 20/stove/telephone) at the start of the Heaphy Track. Collingwood has a motor camp if you wish to spend the night.

Finishing the track at the Kohaihai Shelter (telephone), you may ring up Karamea Motors, a taxi service, for the 15 kilometre ride into Karamea.

THE TRACK

The 77 kilometre/four to five day tramp, popular with families with some experience, is rated easy. It may be walked in either direction, but many prefer to begin in the east, putting the climb up to Perry Saddle behind them on the first day, and leaving the scenic coastline for last. Those walking from west to east, should allow more time for the climb from Lewis to Mackay, and less for the descent between Perry Saddle and Brown Hut.

BROWN HUT (122m) to PERRY SADDLE HUT (868m)
via FLANAGANS CORNER (915m)
5.00 hours, 16km

Elevation:	Moderate
Terrain:	Bush, grassland

From Brown Hut, cross the Brown River on a footbridge and follow the track across the pasture to the start of the climb up to Perry Saddle. The many footbridges on the Heaphy Track have removed much of the flood danger. The track crosses a spur with views down to the Aorere Valley, and eases a bit when an old packhorse track is reached. The climb continues up over numerous ridges in beech forest. In 90 minutes from Brown Hut, you'll reach the turnoff to Shakespeare Flat (400m). Take a right turn and continue climbing for 2 more hours to the Aorere Shelter (sleeps 4/emergency only) where there are nice views down the valley. The track climbs gently now to Flanagans Corner (915m), the high point of the entire track. It's 100 metres to the lookout for views of the Aorere, Mt Olympus, and the Douglas Range. The Perry Saddle Hut (sleeps 25/gas) is 3 kilometres and 45 minutes along a gentle descent.

PERRY SADDLE (868m) to GOULAND DOWNS HUT (610m)
2.00 hours, 8km

Elevation: Gradual
Terrain: Bush, grassland

From the hut, the track climbs a short rise as it winds through beech forest. Shortly, the track opens up to the grasslands of Gouland Downs, with fine views to the expansive rolling tussock-covered hills. From the viewpoint, you turn south and cross Sheep Creek, and later Cave Brook on a footbridge. Look here for the famed Blue Duck, which can often be found in its waters. You'll come next to the older Gouland Downs Hut (sleeps 12) which was built in 1936, and retains its original character. The seemingly silent Downs come to life after dark, when kiwi and weka may call out. If you wander among the Downs, watch carefully for potholes.

GOULAND DOWNS HUT (610m) to SAXON HUT (670m)
1.45 hours, 6km

Elevation: Gradual
Terrain: Bush, grassland

Crossing the northern part of the Downs, the track drops imperceptibly as you cross bridged Shiner Brook, Big River, and Weka Creek. Climbing a bit beyond Weka Creek you can look back across the Downs to Perry Saddle. Walking now along the edge of the bush in less than an hour you'll arrive at the modern Saxon Hut (sleeps 20/gas). You'll find the area the home of numerous keas and wekas as well.

SAXON HUT (670m) to JAMES MACKAY HUT (695m)
via HIGH POINT (750m)
3.30 hours, 11 km

Elevation: Gradual
Terrain: Bush; grassland

About 1 kilometre after Saxon, a high water route branches north. It's advisable to use this route in wet weather since this section can be quite boggy. The track then climbs slowly to a high point below Mt Teddy. Soon you enter the rolling grasslands of Mackay Downs, walking a bit on boardwalks, as the track descends slowly to James Mackay Hut (sleeps 40/gas), hidden on an eastern knoll a bit above the track. From the veranda, you'll get your first views of the Tasman Sea on the West Coast.

JAMES MACKAY HUT (695m) to HEAPHY HUT (5m)
via LEWIS HUT (15m)
6.00 hours, 20km

Elevation: Moderate
Terrain: Bush, riparian
Special Features: Coast views

You enter the bush just after leaving the hut and descend steadily to the West Coast. After 3 to 4 hours, with only a few breaks in the bush, the long 12 kilometre descent finally breaks free at Lewis Hut (sleeps 40/gas) at the confluence of the Heaphy and Lewis Rivers.

Mt Cook from Copland Emergency Shelter, Copland Track

One half a kilometre from Lewis Hut, the track crosses the Heaphy River on a swingbridge to the river's true left side. In 3 kilometres the track crosses Gunner Creek on another swingbridge, a fine stop for lunch or a swim. This is a lovely section as limestone bluffs on the west and the river on the east confine the tramper to the track. After about 2 hours, the track approaches a sandy flat near the river, you'll see your first nikau palms, the majestic tree characteristic of this area. As the nikau thicken, you close in on the Heaphy lagoon, and the track surprisingly opens up to greet the Heaphy Hut (sleeps 40/gas). The beach is not far away, but swimming in the sea is dangerous.

HEAPHY HUT (5m) to KOHAIHAI SHELTER (sea level)
4.30 hours, 16km

Elevation:	Almost level
Terrain:	Coastline
Special Features:	Coast views

Today's walk is undoubtedly one of the South Island's loveliest. Walking along the coast not far from the pounding Tasman Sea will be for many the highlight of the entire trip. Some trampers may avoid the track and instead walk along the actual shore. If they do, they must be cautious as the surf can be dangerous. Lives have been lost by trampers trying to skirt some of the bluffs, especially Crayfish Point, and it is dangerous to walk too close to the high water and surf. Study the tidetables at Heaphy Hut before you set out.

From the Heaphy Hut, you'll head across the sand dunes which are surrounded by palms and in 15 minutes passes the Heaphy Shelter (sleeps 4/emergency only). Continuing through groves of nikau palms, you'll come to the bridged Wekakura Creek and soon the Katipo Creek bridge, often regarded as the day's halfway point. The shelter on the far side of the Creek is a good lunch spot. Just after

Mt Sefton, Copland Track

Twin Beach is the infamous Crayfish Point, where for most trampers safety dictates that you take the high route. Further south, you'll come to the third bridge above Swan Burn and arrive at Scotts Camp, on a grassy clearing 2 kilometres from the road end. Finally, you'll climb gently over a saddle, cross the Kohaihai River on your final swingbridge, and arrive at the road end. You may call a taxi from the public phone at the shelter.

ADDITIONAL INFORMATION

Gas heaters have been added on a trial basis to some of the huts on the Heaphy Track. If they continue to be successful, others may be added in the future.

WANGAPEKA TRACK

The ruggedness and isolation of the Wangapeka Track appeals to only 1500 trampers each year. Passing through North West Nelson State Forest Park south of the Heaphy Track, it crosses bush laden saddles while following several river valleys.

HISTORY

After gold was first discovered in the Wangapeka River Valley in 1859, the valley was opened up as access to the West Coast. In 1862, the rough track was cut from Rolling River, up the Wangapeka River, over the Saddle to the Karamea River to open up the area for gold diggers. A couple of years later, the track was continued on to the site of the present day Taipo Hut, and then zig-zagged up to the Little Wanganui Saddle.

On the western side, after the discovery of gold in Karamea in 1861, a rough track was cut from the Karamea River to the Little Wanganui Valley. Work progressed slowly, and by 1899 the track passed through the Little Wanganui gorge, up Mossy Creek, and over Mt Zetland. The 1929 earthquake obliterated sections of the track on the western sides of Little Wanganui Saddle, and in the Taipo and Upper Karamea Valleys. The Mt Zetland sections of the track were destroyed. In the 1930s, after extensive work, these sections were reopened.

In the 1950s and early 1960s, Luna, Stag Flat, Stone Creek, and Helicopter Flat huts were built. The modern-style huts of Kings Creek, Taipo and Little Wanganui came later. In the Little Wanganui Valley, the Belltown Hut was built by local residents in 1950 and later enlarged by the Forest Service. The neighbouring Little Wanganui Hut later took its place, and the Belltown Hut was demolished. In 1965, after the formation of North West Nelson State Forest Park, the track was repaired and cleared, and bridges and signs were erected.

TRACK ACCESS

Although access to the Wangapeka Track is complicated, it has in recent years become more efficient. To get to the track from Nelson and Motueka take SH 61 to Tapawera. Follow the yellow signs to Tadmor up the Wangapeka Valley on a dirt road. The Dart River, 8 kilometres from the true start of the track, may be difficult for vehicles to ford, and, possibly, you will have to begin or end your walk here. If you can continue on the road, you'll find a car park, Department of Conservation base, telephone, and intentions book at the end of the road, one kilometre from Rolling River and official start of the track.

If Nelson is your starting point, you now have several transport options. On demand van services provided by North West Nelson Trampers Service or Tourist Transport will take you right to the track at Rolling River. These services can be arranged at your convenience. The more riders you have, the less the expense. It pays to call around to assess rates. Wadsworth Motors, a local freight service, departs Nelson daily to Tapawera. They have a taxi service connecting from Tapawera to Rolling River.

From the western track end, it's 3 kilometres to a public phone and vehicle access point, and 8 kilometres total to SH 67. You may wish to call a taxi, Karamea Motors, to take you the 25 kilometres to

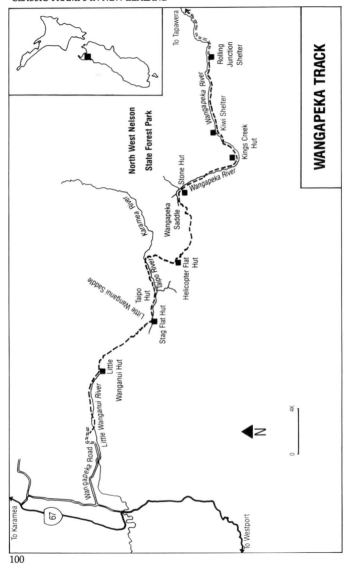

North West Nelson State Forest Park

To Tapawera

Rolling Junction Shelter

Wangapeka River

Kiwi Shelter

Kings Creek Hut

Wangapeka River

Stone Hut

Wangapeka Saddle

Karamea River

Helicopter Flat Hut

Taipo Hut

Taipo River

Little Wanganui Saddle

Stag Flat Hut

Little Wanganui Hut

Little Wanganui River

Wangapeka Road

To Karamea

67

To Westport

WANGAPEKA TRACK

N

0   4K

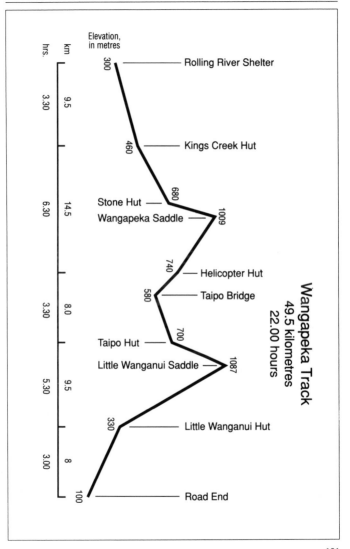

Elevation, in metres

hrs. | km

Rolling River Shelter — 300

3.30 | 9.5

Kings Creek Hut — 460

680

Stone Hut — 680
Wangapeka Saddle — 1009

6.30 | 14.5

740

Helicopter Hut — 740

Taipo Bridge — 580

3.30 | 8.0

Taipo Hut — 700

Little Wanganui Saddle — 1087

5.30 | 9.5

Little Wanganui Hut — 330

3.00 | 8

Road End — 100

Wangapeka Track
49.5 kilometres
22.00 hours

Tramper on swingbridge, Wangapeka Track

Karamea, or the 87 kilometres to Westport, a considerable expense. Cunninghams Coaches runs bus services 6 days a week from Karamea to Westport (and return) where connections can be made to InterCity bus lines to Nelson, Greymouth and the Glaciers, or from Greymouth via the Trans-Alpine Express to Christchurch. If you continue on Cunninghams Coaches to Springs Junction, you may connect to Mount Cook Landlines coach service to Christchurch.

THE TRACK

The track is a 49.5-kilometre four to five day trip with a rating of strenuous. Kings Creek, Taipo and Little Wanganui Huts have gas burners, but you'll need a cooker for the other huts. Though the track may be walked in either direction, the climbs are somewhat easier when approached from the east, beginning at Rolling River.

ROLLING RIVER (300m) to KINGS CREEK HUT (460m)
3.30 hours, 9.5km

Elevation:	Gradual
Terrain:	Bush, grassland, riparian

From the car park, it's 1 kilometre along a dirt road to the official start of the track and the Rolling River Shelter (4 bunks). You first cross Rolling River on a swingbridge to the true right of the Wangapeka River. Meandering along the grassland for $1^1/_2$ hours total, you'll reach the turnoff to Gibbs Creek in 30 minutes, and Patriarch Creek in $1^1/_4$ hours. After entering the bush, it's another $1^1/_2$ hours to the dilapidated Kiwi Shelter (sleeps 4), which can be used in an emergency. Cross the swingbridge to the true left of the river and in another 30 minutes, you'll reach the modern Kings Creek Hut (sleeps 20/gas/stove) in a clearing not far from the river. Five minutes farther on the track, you'll find the historic and restored Kings Hut (4 bunks) built for gold prospecting in 1935 by Cecil King.

KINGS CREEK HUT (460m) to STONE HUT (680m)
2.30 hours, 6.5km

Elevation:	Gradual
Terrain:	Bush, riparian

The track travels above the north branch of the Wangapeka River for 2 hours, a lovely river walk through forests with moss hanging from the trees. Crossing over a bridge to the river's true right just after Luna Stream, it's another 30 minutes to the older Stone Hut (sleeps 6) in a nice clearing beside Stone Creek.

STONE HUT (680m) to HELICOPTER FLAT HUT (740m)
via WANGAPEKA SADDLE (1009m)
4.0 hours, 8km

Elevation:	Parts steep, parts moderate
Terrain:	Bush, riparian
Special Features:	River crossings

Leaving Stone Hut, the track crosses open flats on the river's true right weaving across strewn boulders that testify to the 1929 Murchison earthquake. In 30 minutes, you enter the bush and climb steeply to the Wangapeka Saddle, about 75 minutes from the hut. There is water a few minutes before the saddle, and you'll enjoy a rest stop in the clearing next to the rain gauge.

At the saddle, a track heads north to Biggs Top and descends steeply to Luna Hut. From here, you can rejoin the Wangapeka Track by crossing the Taipo River to Trevor Carter Hut and walking down the river to the Taipo Bridge. Another track from the saddle also heads south to Nugget Knob. For both tracks, it's about 1 hour from the saddle to the bushline.

Descending steeply from the saddle past Chime Creek, you may, if the water level is high, have to use the walkwire. In 45 minutes you'll reach the Karamea River Valley and you must ford to the true left of the river. The high water route avoids the river crossings and remains on the river's true left, adding 20 minutes to your time. If you choose the river route, after crossing twice more, you'll reach the older Helicopter Flat Hut in about 30 minutes (sleeps 6/stove) located on the bank of the river.

HELICOPTER FLAT HUT (740m) to TAIPO HUT (700m) via TAIPO RIVER BRIDGE (580m)
3.30 hours, 8km

Elevation:	Gradual
Terrain:	Bush, riparian

Sidling above the Karamea River for an hour, the track comes to the Tabernacle Lookout, where there are striking views east to the junction of the Taipo and Karamea Rivers. Here there is little left of a former A-frame structure used during track construction in the late 1890s. Less than 5 minutes past the overlook, a side track drops to the east to join the confluence of these two rivers. Following this, you may venture up the Karamea to Luna or Trevor Carter Huts and later rejoin the Wangapeka Track on the Taipo River Track by traversing the northern shore or true left of the river.

Half an hour beyond the turn off to Luna Hut, the track descends moderately to the Taipo River swingbridge (580m). Crossing the river, the well-marked track climbs gradually on the river's true left for 2 hours to reach the modern Taipo Hut (sleeps 12/gas/stove).

TAIPO HUT (700m) to LITTLE WANGANUI HUT (330m) via STAG FLAT HUT (945m) and LITTLE WANGANUI SADDLE (1087m)
5.30 hours, 9.5km

Elevation:	Steep
Terrain:	Bush, riparian
Special Features:	River crossings; valley views, coast views

From Taipo Hut, the track climbs 245 metres steadily upwards for 1 hour to the dilapidated Stag Flat Hut (4 bunks/emergency use) located in the middle of a boggy meadow. There are views back down to the Taipo River Valley from the knoll above the hut. The track climbs again for 30 minutes to the 1087 metre Little Wanganui Saddle, where there are nice views back to Stag Flat, and if the weather is clear, to the Saddle Lakes and West Coast. From the saddle, you drop steeply over rocky sections where care is required in wet weather. This section may be difficult for inexperienced or less fit trampers. After descending 450 metres for about 2 hours to meet the Little Wanganui River, you'll cross to the true right on a footbridge. An hour later, the track begins its descent through the Wanganui Gorge. The gorge should only be attempted in low water, and by parties experienced in river crossings. A total of four river crossings are necessary, and it may be necessary to link arms with other trampers or use a sturdy pole for mutual support. The water may be too deep and swift for a solo tramper. Take care to look for cairns, track markings on the river's opposite side and signs reading "Ford". The high water route remains on the river's true right, and involves a steep climb, but is considerably safer. If in any doubt, use it. Just after the high and low tracks merge, a swingbridge to the river's true left leads to the Little Wanganui Hut (sleeps 16/gas/stove), at the site of the old Belltown Hut. If travelling from west to east, you need to plan an extra hour for the climb.

LITTLE WANGANUI HUT (330m) to ROAD END (100m)
3.00 hours, 8km

Elevation:	Gradual
Terrain:	Bush, grassland, riparian
Special Features:	River crossings

From the hut, cross back to the river's true right on the swingbridge and follow the track west. The low water route requires four separate river crossings. In high water or wet weather, you should choose the longer but safer high water route. On the low-water

Trampers near Stag Flat Hut, Wangapeka Track

route, you cross grassy river flats as you follow the poles which mark the track. Finally you join up with an old logging road which connects with the road end. Don't forget to sign out here. Three kilometres more down the old road to a vehicle access point and a telephone gives you time to savour the last moments on track and look back to the bush clad mountains you've just crossed. From the telephone, you are still 5 kilometres from SH 67, and 25 kilometres south of Karamea.

COMBINATION WALKS

A pleasurable ten day holiday combines the Heaphy and the Wangapeka Tracks, resupplying in Karamea. Even better, if you have the time, first walk the Abel Tasman Coast Track. Using the bus or launch services, complete your trip in either Takaka or Motueka. From here you can resupply and catch another coach to Collingwood and the Heaphy Track. Return walking west to east on the Wangapeka, but before you depart arrange for a pick up at Rolling River to take you back to your starting point at the conclusion of your tramp.

CONTACTS

Department of Conservation:

Nelson - Monro Building, Bridge St, Private Bag, Nelson
0-3-546 9335
Motueka - Cnr King Edward and High St, PO Box 97, Motueka
0-3 528 9117
Karamea - Main Road, PO Box 47, Karamea   0-3-782 6852
Takaka - PO Box 53, Takaka   0-3-525 8026

Information Centres *(i)*:

Nelson - Nelson Visitor Centre, Cnr Trafalgar and Halifax Sts,
  PO Box 194, Nelson   0-3-548 2304
Motueka - 236 High Street, Motueka   0-3-528 6543
Karamea - Waverly Street, Karamea   0-3-782 6617

Transport:

Abel Tasman National Park Enterprises, Main Road, Motueka,
RD 3, Nelson   0-3-528 7801
Collingwood Bus Services, c/o Post Office, Collingwood
                                                       0-3-524 8188
Cunninghams Coaches, Westport   0-3-789 7177
Golden Bay Connection, Nelson: contact Nelson Visitor Centre, Cnr
   Traflagar and Halifax Sts, Nelson   0-3-548 8369
Karamea Motors, No 1 RD, Karamea   0-3-782 6757
North West Nelson Trampers Service, 145 Thorp St, Motueka
                                                       0-3-528 9120
Tourist Transport, 33 Paremata St, Nelson   0-3-545 1055
Skyline Travel, Nelson   0-3-548 0285
Wadsworth Motors, Tapawera   0-3-522 4248

CHAPTER 11: SOUTH ISLAND, NORTH CENTRAL: NELSON LAKES NATIONAL PARK

TRAVERS-SABINE LOOP VIA MT ROBERT

This towering snow-dazzled-sun-shot world
Of rock on rock, mountain on mountain hurled
Cupping cold lakes, bare valleys curved for sleep.

Charles Brasch on Nelson Lakes

The great range of the Southern Alps running a large part of the length of the South Island extends from its southern Fiordland peaks to Nelson Lakes, where the high peaks are last seen. Here lush valleys with swift-flowing rivers are linked by high alpine passes. Two long narrow lakes, Rotoroa ("long lake") and Rotoiti ("small lake"), remnants of vanishing glaciers, provide a majestic setting for these towering peaks. Of the mountain ranges which surround the park, to the east is the St Arnaud Range, to the south the Spenser Mountains, and to the west the Ella Range. The northern peaks are between 1200 and 1800 metres, and the southern ones rise to about 2100 metres. Three rivers, the Travers, which flows into Lake Rotoiti, and the Sabine and D'Urville which flow into Lake Rotoroa, divide the park. The area attracts many on holiday for boating and swimming. Lake Rotoiti may be the more popular of the two, but Lake Rotoroa perhaps the more beautiful.

Trampers soon will discover a park known for high alpine walks with a milder climate than the southern mountains. Those wishing to avoid crowds will be enthusiastic about Nelson Lakes where a feeling of wildness and ruggedness pervades the senses. Trampers should know that the tracks, though well-maintained, are not the typical manicured trails such as on the Milford or Routeburn. Though distances may be short on some tracks, elevation gain is often great, and plenty of time should be allowed. Routes over the passes may be poled, cairned or not marked at all. Due to these factors, previous tramping experience is highly recommended.

WEATHER

Considering the high mountains which surrounded this area, its climate is surprisingly mild. Rain does blow in from the Tasman Sea leaving much more precipitation in the western Sabine and D'Urville Valleys. The Travers Valley is drier than the west as its average annual rainfall is about 2000 millimetres per year. Early morning fog is common along the ridges and through the passes. The tramper should always be prepared for winter conditions, carry a couple of days extra food, and allow for weather delay. As is true with all mountain areas in New Zealand, conditions can change rapidly.

BASE

St Arnaud (population 200), 119 kilometres SSW of Nelson and 103 kilometres SW of Blenheim on SH 6, boasts a lovely setting at the northern end of Lake Rotoiti beneath the Robert Ridge and St Arnaud Range. The area draws vacationers from all over New Zealand for boating, tramping, and skiing. This tiny town has a small store, tearoom, petrol station, post office, and the Nelson Lakes National Park Headquarters.

In St Arnaud, there is limited but adequate accommodation. There is a reasonably priced 20-unit modern motel on nice grounds, and next door but down the street, a very friendly backpacker's accommodation. Lake Rotoroa and Rotoiti both have campgrounds.

HISTORY

The first European to have visited Lake Rotoiti was John Cotterell, who first came upon the lake in 1843 as he journeyed from Nelson searching for farmland. Later explorers, looking for gold, in 1846 crossed the mountains to discover Lake Rotoroa. Although some of the early explorers considered the land to be totally useless, Julius Von Haast wrote about Lake Rotoiti in 1860: "its deep blue waters reflected the high mountain chains on its eastern and southern shores which for a considerable height from the water's edge are clad with luxuriant primeval forest". Haast found only a small amount of gold, but it was enough to kindle expectations. The track used by the gold-seekers became SH 6 in 1920. Ten years later a connecting road was built to Lake Rotoiti and St Arnaud. The park itself became the eighth National Park in New Zealand in 1956, and the Spenser Mountains were added to its jurisdiction in 1982.

TRANSPORT/TRACK ACCESS

There are several bus companies serving St Arnaud. Wadsworth Motors and Nelson Lakes Transport run buses between Nelson and St Arnaud several times a week, with Nelson Lake Transport providing daily service in the summer. Nelson Lakes Transport provides transport from Picton as well. InterCity Bus Lines running between Nelson and Westport, or Newmans buses on the Nelson - Lewis Pass - Christchurch route will let you off at Kawatiri Junction, 20 kilometres west, at the junction of SH 6 and 63. Traffic, however, is light on the road into St Arnaud.

The track begins at the head of Lake Rotoiti, a 5 minute walk from the Nelson Lakes National Park Visitor Centre. Rotoiti Water Taxi provides year-round service to either Coldwater or Lakehead Huts. If you choose to begin by crossing the Robert Ridge, it's a $1^1/_2$ hour uphill walk to the Mt Robert car park. If leaving from the Sabine Hut via the head of Lake Rotoroa, a water taxi is available, but must be reserved. Take note, however, that it may be hard get a lift back to St Arnaud from Lake Rotoroa, a good thirty minutes by car. The park headquarters has information on boat access to the track across either lake.

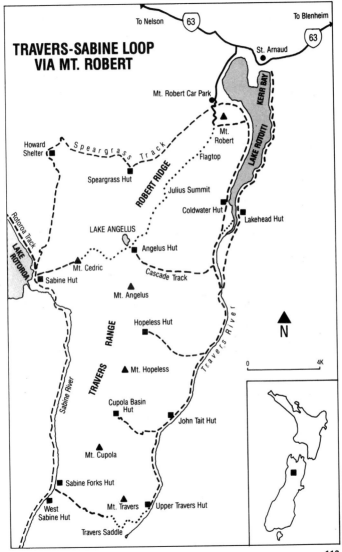

TRAVERS-SABINE LOOP VIA MT. ROBERT

To Nelson

63

To Blenheim

63

St. Arnaud

Mt. Robert Car Park

KERR BAY

Mt. Robert

Flagtop

Howard Shelter

Speargrass Track

ROBERT RIDGE

LAKE ROTOITI

Speargrass Hut

Julius Summit

Coldwater Hut

Lakehead Hut

Rotoroa Track

LAKE ANGELUS

Angelus Hut

LAKE ROTOROA

Mt. Cedric

Cascade Track

Sabine Hut

Mt. Angelus

Travers River

Hopeless Hut

RANGE

N

Sabine River

Mt. Hopeless

TRAVERS

Cupola Basin Hut

John Tait Hut

0   4K

Mt. Cupola

Sabine Forks Hut

West Sabine Hut

Mt. Travers

Upper Travers Hut

Travers Saddle

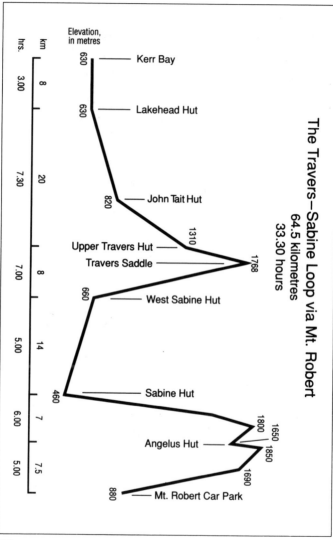

The Travers–Sabine Loop via Mt. Robert
64.5 kilometres
33.30 hours

Elevation, in metres

hrs.   km

630 — Kerr Bay
3.00   8
630 — Lakehead Hut
7.30   20
820 — John Tait Hut
1310
Upper Travers Hut
Travers Saddle
7.00   8   1768
660 — West Sabine Hut
5.00   14
460 — Sabine Hut
6.00   7   1800   1650
Angelus Hut   1850
5.00   7.5   1690
880 — Mt. Robert Car Park

TRAVERS-SABINE LOOP VIA ANGELUS HUT

The Travers-Sabine Loop is one of Nelson Lakes' most popular tramps. Numerous variations allow you to start or finish with a unparalleled tramp across the Mt Robert Ridge to the Angelus Hut.

Many different combinations of walks are possible. I have described a six to seven day 64.5 kilometre strenuous route that begins at Kerr Bay, ascends the gentle Travers Valley to the John Tait Hut and Travers Saddle Hut and crosses over the Travers Saddle. The route then descends to the Sabine Valley. From the Sabine Hut, the route climbs over Mt Cedric to the spectacular Angelus Hut and exits via the Mt Robert Ridge. You may begin by traversing the Mt Robert Ridge, and dropping into the Travers Valley or the Sabine. If you are feeling less ambitious, try a lovely three to four day walk up the Travers Valley with a day hike to the Travers Saddle. Return by retracing your steps to St Arnaud, or add some variety by exiting via the Coldwater Hut and the Lakeside Track on the western side of Lake Rotoiti. Lovely side trips to either Hopeless or Cupola Basin Huts are good alternatives as well.

KERR BAY (630m) to LAKEHEAD HUT (630m)
3.00 hours, 8km

Elevation:	Almost level
Terrain:	Bush, riparian
Special Features:	Mountain views

Starting at Kerr Bay near the Park Headquarters, follow the Loop Track along the east side of Lake Rotoiti, the most direct route around the lake from St Arnaud. After a kilometre, you join the true track and continue to skirt the lake through forest. At 4 and 7 kilometres the track emerges from the forest for good views of the lake. Rest at any of the many bays you pass on route. The Lakehead Hut (sleeps 16 / stove) is at the south end of the lake near the mouth of the Travers River. Jet boat service to either Lakehead Hut or

Coldwater Hut (sleeps 6) is available. If you are heading up the valley that day, the more direct route is from the Coldwater Hut. The Travers Valley may also be reached from the eastern shore of the lake on the track connecting to the Mt Robert car park.

LAKEHEAD HUT (630m) to JOHN TAIT HUT (820m)
4.30 hours, 13km

Elevation:	Almost level
Terrain:	Bush, riparian
Special Features:	Mountain views

From Lakehead Hut, follow the trail on the true right of the river up the broad flats. If the river is low, you may be able to ford across the river inlet and cross to the western side, a more direct route up the valley. It takes about 1½ hours to cover the 5 kilometres to the swingbridge to the western side of the river. From the swingbridge, cross to the true left of the river and wander up the lovely valley, where you will find numerous campsites in the grassy clearings. Soon Mt Travers will come into view at the far end of the valley, and you pass the side track to Hopeless Hut 1½ hours and 3½ kilometres from the swingbridge. Five kilometres more in and out of forest brings you to roomy John Tait Hut (sleep 15/stove) located in a grassy clearing near the river with splendid views of the peak. Good campsites can be found in the clearing around the hut.

If travelling up the valley on the true left of the river from the Coldwater Hut, you will come in an hour to the Cascade Creek turn off to Lake Angelus, next to Hukere Stream. This difficult steep 1000 metre ascent to the Angeles Basin follows the true right of the stream. Quietly beautiful, except for the roar of the tumbling creek, you pass numerous cascades surrounded by mountain ridges in a tangled beech forest. Allow 5 hours for the 8-kilometre ascent to Angelus Hut from either Lakehead or Coldwater Hut.

JOHN TAIT HUT (820m) to UPPER TRAVERS HUT (1310m)
3.00 hours, 7km

Elevation:	Steep
Terrain:	Bush, riparian
Special Features:	Mountain views

About 15 minutes walking will bring you to the first swingbridge and the turn-off up Cupola Creek to Cupola Basin Hut. Continue on another 40 minutes to the Summit Creek footbridge. You may wish to take a break here for a short detour to Travers waterfall. Returning to the main track, the valley narrows and the climb steepens. In 2 kilometres you come out of the bush and enter a tussock covered flat with rocks and a roaring stream. The two room Upper Travers Hut (sleeps 16/stove) sits at the far end in a splendid setting. Early morning fog inching between the neighbouring peaks makes for a lovely photo.

UPPER TRAVERS HUT (1310m) to WEST SABINE HUT or SABINE FORKS HUT (660m) via TRAVERS SADDLE (1768m)
6-9 hours (depending on snow conditions), 8km

Elevation:	Parts extremely steep, parts gradual
Terrain:	Grassland, bush
Special Features:	Mountain pass, mountain views

Since the weather is more settled in the morning, it is advisable to start early. Good visibility is required as the pass cannot be seen from the hut. Follow the path leading across the stream next to the hut, and begin a poled ascent northward up a scree slope. This leads in 1 hour to a tarned rocky basin below the base of triangular Mt Travers. An additional 30 minutes of walking is needed to cross to the top of the pass, a total of 458 metres above the hut.

Almost immediately, you begin a steep loose 300-metre descent to the bushline. In most places a faint trail can be located but over the rocky areas poles lead the way, though these may be flattened by avalanches. From the bushline the route follows a steep rocky stream bed, at first on the true right and crossing to its true left midway. Watch carefully for the cairns and poles since the area is prone to avalanches and the actual track route may differ somewhat from the description. You will find the true track at the bottom of the gully along the East Branch of the Sabine. After 15 minutes on the valley floor, you cross the footbridge above a gorge plunging 30 metres into the river. You've descended 600 metres since the bushline! It's 3 more kilometres and 1 hour in heavy bush to a steep drop off 175 metres down to the Sabine River. The weathered Sabine Forks Hut (sleeps 8/stove) is located in bush across the swingbridge on the true left of the river. You'll find the West Sabine Hut (sleeps 8/stove) 10 minutes farther along in a pleasant clearing past the second swingbridge. If you have an extra day, you may find the trip up to Blue Lake worthwhile.

SABINE FORKS/WEST SABINE HUTS (660m) to SABINE HUT at LAKE ROTOROA (460m)
5.00 hours, 14km

Elevation:	Almost level, short parts steep
Terrain:	Bush, riparian

Return to the swingbridge and cross to the true left of the Sabine River where you will find relatively easy tramping for much of the day. The track winds in and out of beech forest, at times coming close to the water and traversing the flats. Only at the far end later in the day, you do veer away from the river and climb a small saddle. This exertion will be demanding if you are still weary from your crossing of the Travers Saddle! After returning to the river, the track branches to the left heading to the D'Urville Hut. Take the right branch if heading for the Sabine Hut and cross the bridge high above the rocky gorge. Look for trout in the swirling river below you, or for a sidelined tramper who decided to stop for a swim! Once out on the grassy flats you've only a kilometre more to the Sabine Hut (sleeps 12/stove) on a pleasing spot on the edge of Lake

Rotoroa but quite popular with the sandflies as well. From here, there is water taxi service to the head of Lake Rotoroa (reservations necessary).

Three different routes take you back to Lake Rotoiti. You may follow along the eastern shore of Lake Rotoroa to its head, or follow the Howard Valley to Speargrass Creek. The most scenic and most demanding route is a climb up over Mt Cedric to Lake Angelus Hut followed by a trek over Robert Ridge to Lake Rotoiti. A description of each route follows below.

SABINE HUT (460m) to HEAD OF LAKE ROTOROA (460m)
6.00 hours, 11km

Elevation:	Rolling
Terrain:	Bush, riparian

Here the track follows the eastern side of Lake Rotoroa totally in bush. The trip to the head of the lake, up and down numerous small gullies, can be tedious, and transport back to Lake Rotoroa difficult. It is, however, a wilder, quieter place than Lake Rotoiti. Trout fisherman know well of its virtues. The protected New Zealand bird, the scaup, may be spotted here.

SABINE HUT (460m) to MT ROBERT CAR PARK (880m)
via SPEARGRASS HUT(1070m)
9.00 hours,18km

Elevation:	Gradual, parts steep
Terrain:	Bush, grassland, riparian

From the Sabine Hut, follow the track 6 kilometres toward Howard Valley to the Howard Shelter (sleeps 4). You will need another 3 hours for the steep 600 metre ascent to the Speargrass Hut (sleeps 6/stove), 12 kilometres total from the Sabine Hut. From the hut, follow the Speargrass Creek 6 kilometres to the Mt Robert car park. It is also possible to follow the Speargrass Creek to the Mt Robert ridge, although there is no track.

SABINE HUT (460m) to ANGELUS HUT (1650m)
via MT CEDRIC (1532m) and HIGH POINT (1800m)
6.00 hours, 7km

Elevation:	Extremely steep, parts steep
Terrain:	Bush; scrub
Special Features:	Mountain views

Start today by filling your water bottle as you will find no water en route. The track begins very steeply right behind the hut, and you will gain 1000 metres in a bit more than 4 kilometres. After leaving the bushline, the track changes to a poled route. At the top of Mt Cedric (1532m), you will have a sweeping view of Lake Rotoroa and the surrounding mountains. From here, follow the snow poles over the ridge to the high point at 1650 metres and continue to follow the ridge south. Next, circle a basin with a small tarn that supplies the Cedric stream. Cross the ridge at 1800 metres heading east before beginning the drop into the Angelus Basin. After sighting the hut, it is still another 20 minutes to the bright orange Angelus hut (sleeps 40/gas heater/summer warden) recently upgraded and enlarged. The poles follow around the outlet from the two lakes to the hut.

ANGELUS HUT (1650m) to MT ROBERT CAR PARK (880m)
via ROBERT RIDGE HIGH POINT(1850m)
5.00 hours, 7.5km

Elevation:	Steep, parts extremely steep
Terrain:	Bush, scrub
Special Features:	Mountain views

Provided the "tops" are clear, the route back to Lake Rotoiti along

Signpost, Travers-Sabine Loop via Mt Robert

the Robert Ridge is as fine a ridge walk as there is in New Zealand. Walk north from the hut around the eastern shore of the lake and for half a kilometre ascend a 180 metre scree slope to a saddle overlooking the Angelus Basin, Mt Angelus, and the Sunset Saddle. From the saddle, the day's high point, drop down to the col (1814m) to begin your traverse of the fourth basin overlooking Shift Creek. Follow the poled route carefully, as you criss-cross the Robert Ridge. The rocky areas require a bit of scrambling and may be difficult for inexperienced trampers. Speargrass Creek, which can be used as an alternative exit from the ridge in poor weather, winds from its higher tarns all the way to Speargrass Hut. On a clear day you can see all the way to the hut. Upon reaching the saddle (1794m) near Julius Summit, the route descends gradually along the ridge of the third basin to Flagtop (1690m). Now, high above the Mt Robert skifield, traverse the second basin around the ski tows, dropping gradually again 180 metres to Christie Lodge. From above the lodge, join the Pinchgut Track descending to the Relax Emergency Shelter and the turn off to Paddys Track and the Bushline Hut. Descend the final 500 metres past the Bushedge Shelter over the face of Mt Robert to the Mt Robert car park. If you want an extra night in the mountains, take the short 1 kilometre detour to the new hut, where there are fine views of the lake. You may be able to hitch a ride from the car park back to town, since you are still about 5 kilometres from St Arnaud via the West Bay Road. Otherwise, you face another 1¼ hours on foot.

CONTACTS:

Department of Conservation:

Nelson Lakes National Park, St Arnaud	0-3-521 1806
Rotoiti Water Taxi, Bill Butters, St Arnaud	0-3-521 1894
Nelson Lakes Transport, Main Road, St Arnaud	0-3-521 1858
Wadsworth Motors, Main Road, Tapawera	0-3-522 4248
Visitor Information (i) Nelson, Cnr Trafalgar and Halifax Sts,	
PO Box 194, Nelson	0-3-548 2304

CHAPTER 12: SOUTH ISLAND, CENTRAL: MOUNT COOK NATIONAL PARK

COPLAND TRACK

The magnificent pyramid of Mt Cook, or Aorangi, stood high
above all, towering into the sky. As far as the eye could
reach everywhere snow and ice and rock appeared around
us, and in such gigantic proportions that sometimes I
thought I was dreaming.

Julius von Haast - 1862

Mount Cook is the centre of the great range of New Zealand's southern Alps. Stretching from Nelson, in the north, all the way to Fiordland in the south, the chain of peaks ranks as one of the world's most rugged ranges. Twenty-seven peaks exceed 3000 metres, and, though these heights may not be terribly impressive by world standards, the combined challenge of glaciation, tremendous vertical rise, and unpredictable, unforgiving weather makes the area irresistible to climbers. At 3753.5 metres,[1] Mt Cook is New Zealand's highest peak. Its triangular ridge dominates the eastern skyline. Mt Sefton, at 3159 metres, seems to tower over the tiny Mt Cook Village, as its eastern face rises 2400 metres above the valley floor and sounds of frequent avalanches are heard down the valley. Mt Tasman, at 3498 metres, thought by many to be one of the world's most beautiful peaks, presents a serious mountaineering challenge.

Mt Cook's glaciers add much to its distinctiveness. The Hooker Glacier flows from the western slopes of Mt Cook. The Franz Josef and Fox Glaciers extend west from the main divide into Westland National Park and appear to drop precipitously into the Tasman

---

[1] In December, 1991 a massive avalanche on the eastern face of Mt Cook forever altered the shape and height of the mountain. The Mountain lost 10.4 metres in height and now measures 3753.5 metres.

Sea. The Tasman Glacier, 29 kilometres long and 3 kilometres wide, dominates the eastern side of the park, where its icy tables meet the vertical ridges of the Alps. The smaller Hooker Glacier and Mueller Glaciers are visible from the Copland Pass.

Because of its forbidding snow and ice, Mount Cook is more of a mountaineer's rather than a tramper's park. But don't let that discourage you from visiting this high mountain wonderland. The Copland Track, rated expert, can be accomplished by advanced trampers if accompanied by a guide. There are few places where one encounters scenery of such variety in so short a span of time. In four days, you pass from majestic glaciers, over a true alpine pass to the grandeur of the Copland Valley, soothe your sore muscles in superb hot pools, and cross through rainforest and bush.

WEATHER

Mount Cook National Park has some of the harshest weather in all of New Zealand. The high peaks make their own weather. Without warning, fierce storms may envelop the area, bringing freezing temperatures, snow, and high winds. Long periods of unsettled weather are common in springtime, but not unknown at any time of year. On the other hand, there can also be extended periods of fine weather, especially in late summer and mid-winter. Be sure to listen to the evening weather reports on the hut radio, and check the forecast before departing from Mount Cook Village. Careful attention to the weather forecast is one of the keys to a successful crossing of the Copland Pass.

BASE

It is strongly recommended that you begin your tramp in Mount Cook Village, and travel east to west over the pass. The tiny village of Mount Cook, population 200, is located 106 kilometres NW of Tekapo, and 59 kilometres from Lake Pukaki on SH 80. Here you'll find the National Park Headquarters, a well-stocked store and post office, and, Alpine Guides, a guiding service. Located nearby is the world-famous Hermitage Hotel, a motel and budget accommodation. They are all expensive for what they offer. There is a very nice youth hostel with a central cooking area and large common room. All facilities are heavily booked during the summer, and reservations are essential. There is a small charge for the White Horse Hill campground, 1¹/₂ kilometres from the village.

On the western side, tiny Fox Glacier has a hotel and pub, motels, several backpacker's lodges and the Westland National Park Visitor Centre. Mount Cook Airline has an office here along with several helicopter companies offering flights over the glaciers, Westland and Mount Cook National Parks. If you wish to return to Mount Cook after your trip and are lucky enough to have good weather, you may wish to charter a plane or a helicopter for the spectacular trans-alpine flight from Fox to Mount Cook.

HISTORY

In the 1890s the Government was anxious to find a connecting route between the tourist centres of Mount Cook and Fox-Franz Josef on the West Coast. Charles Douglas, exploring the west side of the Divide, discovered the hot springs at Welcome Flat. He felt it might be possible to link the two areas with a track over the Copland Pass, although he ruled out the possibility of a road due to the heavy yearly snowfall.

The first recorded east to west crossing of the Divide occurred in 1895, when Fitzgerald and Zurbriggen climbed Fitzgerald Pass, just south of the Copland Pass. Thinking it a short trip down the Copland Valley to accommodation, they consumed all their supplies on the pass. Three arduous days followed, as without food or equipment, they forced their way down the valley. A few weeks later, Arthur P. Harper crossed the Copland Pass, an easier route.

Track construction began in 1910 and extended up to snow level on the west side of the pass. During the early half of the century, the Copland became a popular crossing for experienced mountaineers and guided trampers who would rest for a couple of days on the West Coast in Fox and return to Mt Cook via the Graham Saddle. Welcome Flat Hut was built in 1913 and replaced in 1987. That same year a mud slide filled the new hut, and it was relocated to a safer site several hundred yards upstream from the old location still near the Copland River. The Douglas Rock Hut was built in 1934, near a large bivouac rock that sheltered trampers for many years. The rock has long since been buried by avalanche.

TRANSPORT/TRACK ACCESS

Mount Cook is served by daily buses on InterCity and Mount Cook Landline from Queenstown and Christchurch. Mount Cook Airlines has three or four flights a day from both cities. On a clear day the flight into Mount Cook is spectacular, and passengers are allowed up into the cockpit for a complete view of the Mt Cook Range. The one room Mount Cook Airport boasts its own superb setting not far from the terminal of the Tasman Glacier. A free coach will transport all passengers to Mount Cook Village and the Hermitage Hotel which serves as bus terminal for all arriving and departing coaches. The tourist flights above the National Park are worth every penny.

On the western side, the coast is served daily by InterCity between Fox and Franz Josef and Queenstown. The northbound InterCity bus crosses the Karangarua bridge on SH 6 sometime around mid-afternoon; the southbound bus passes through early morning. Northbound connections to Greymouth and Nelson, and eastward to Christchurch are made the following day. You must signal the bus to stop. In addition, backpacker's transport Kiwi Experience serves Fox Glacier. Since traffic is often light, hitchhiking is not reliable in this area. You should check the bus schedules before you leave Mount Cook.

THE TRACK

This three to four day 46 kilometre crossing of the Main Divide of the Southern Alps is rated expert, and previous mountaineering experience or a trained guide is essential. Don't forget that this is a mountaineering venture of the utmost seriousness. Dramatic weather changes occur quickly bringing cloud, wind and snow to the area. Experience in the use of ice axe and crampons is required for all members of your party, and one member should be skillful in the use of a rope. Lives are lost most every year on the Copland usually

Copland Valley, Copland Track

by those who ignore such warnings, or who lack experience to undertake such a trip. Excellent guiding services are available (see below).

The track should be walked from east to west. Not only is the elevation gain less when beginning in Mount Cook Village, but, if travelling from west to east, trampers can easily mistake the lower but more dangerous Fitzgerald Pass for the Copland Pass. Trampers beginning in the west often reach the Copland Pass in the afternoon, when clouds often obscure the visibility on the Copland Ridge.

The track to the Hooker Hut can be completed as a day walk from Mount Cook Village, or as an overnight trip. If not continuing over the Copland Pass, just retrace your steps back to the village. If crossing over the pass, the Hooker Hut serves as the first overnight shelter

MOUNT COOK VILLAGE (730m) to HOOKER HUT (1120m)
3 hours, 10km

Elevation:	Steep
Terrain:	Grassland, riparian
Special Features:	Glaciers, mountain views, river crossings

Begin your trip by registering your intentions at the Mount Cook National Park Headquarters. Here there are interesting exhibits, a slide show and a relief map of the park. Check here for the latest weather forecast, and information on avalanche hazards. You will want to inquire specifically about the section between the Hooker Hut and the Copland Ridge. This part of the route, especially prone to avalanche and morainal shift, varies from year to year.

You may be able to hitch a ride to the White Horse Hill campground, just north of the village (shelter/toilets). Otherwise, take the Kea Point trail which begins alongside the Hermitage Hotel and after 10 minutes turn right at the junction to the Hooker Valley Trail. The track officially begins next to the memorial to the first three climbers killed on Mt Cook in 1914. The mountain, rising an astounding 2500 metres above the valley floor, comes in and out of view as you proceed away from the village.

Within the first 15 minutes, after wandering through tussocks and open grassland, you will come to the first swingbridge across the Hooker River. You'll lose sight of Mt Cook, but views of Mt Sefton and the Mueller Glacier open up. You cross to the true left of the river, for the next 20 minutes the track sidles above the river, parts of it cut through rock, until it recrosses the river on another swingbridge. Mt Cook comes into view again, its southwestern face no longer obscured by the ridges farther up the valley. In 4 kilometres and a little over 1 hour, still on well formed track, you reach the Stocking Stream Shelter, a popular lunch spot. To the west there is a commanding view of Mt Sefton's glaciers and overhanging icefalls. Even if this is only a day trip, it is well worth the effort to continue on up the valley.

The track then continues another $1^{1}/_{2}$ kilometres over low lying brush to the glacial Hooker Lake. Here the trail passes close to the

Stream, Routeburn Track

Stream crossing on day trip from Dart Hut, Rees-Dart Track

lake where there is an easy stream crossing. You may be able to cross higher up without losing elevation, but high water will complicate crossing here and care should be taken. Past this point, the designation of the track changes to a route. Pay attention to the "No Stopping Avalanche Danger" signs as you continue up the valley through more alpine scrub and some steep scree sections. Though this area may seem desolate, an occasional Mount Cook lily, the huge mountain buttercup, can be seen in the spring and early summer. The track climbs a 50 metre spur, and there are rewarding views southward back to the Hermitage. Next you walk on broad terraces very high above the terminal moraine of the glacier, undulating all the way to the hut. Two more stream crossings, the run-off from the Eugenie and Hayter Glaciers, should be thoughtfully approached especially in the afternoons when water level will be highest. Watch for cairns as you cross the gullies. Slowly you gain elevation, the vegetation thins, and finally from atop the last terrace you sight the cozy Hooker Hut (sleeps 12/primus stoves/radio). Each year the drop off of the moraine moves closer to the hut. Devastating erosive changes in the landscape are common in Mount Cook, and, in the next few years, may necessitate moving the Hooker Hut to a safer location.

HOOKER HUT (1120m) to DOUGLAS ROCK (700m)
via COPLAND EMERGENCY SHELTER (1830m)
and COPLAND PASS (2150m)
8-10 hours, 12km

Elevation:	Extremely steep; parts steep
Terrain:	Scrub, snow, rock
Special Features:	Alpine pass, glaciers, mountain views, technical equipment and mountaineering experience required; river crossings

Plan to leave the hut at first light, usually around 5 a.m., in order to

---

Tramper on walkwire, Hollyford Track

▲ Mt. Cook

Hooker Glacier

Copland Pass

Copland Shelter Hut

Hooker Shelter Hut

Hooker Valley Track

80

To Twizel

Hermitage Hotel

Mt. Cook Village

Hooker River

Stocking Stream

Scott Creek

▲ Mt. Sefton

N

Copland Track

Douglas Rock Hut

Welcome Flat Hut

S I E R R A   R A N G E

Architect Creek

Copland River

4K

0

To Fox Glacier

6

Karangarua River

To Haast

COPLAND TRACK

130

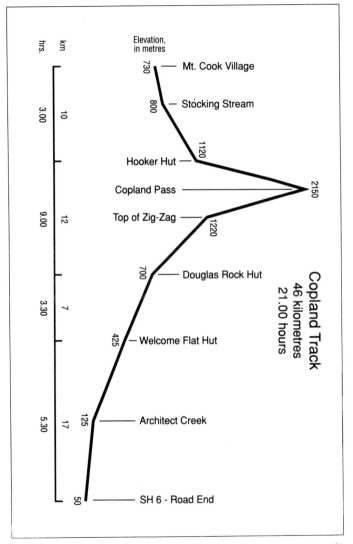

Copland Track
46 kilometres
21.00 hours

Elevation, in metres

730 — Mt. Cook Village

800 — Stocking Stream

1120

Hooker Hut —

Copland Pass — 2150

Top of Zig-Zag — 1220

700 — Douglas Rock Hut

425 — Welcome Flat Hut

125 — Architect Creek

50 — SH 6 - Road End

hrs. | km
3.00 | 10
9.00 | 12
3.30 | 7
5.30 | 17

be on top of the pass as early as possible. Clouds often come in in the early afternoon, and vicious storms can arise, quickly reducing the visibility. From the Hooker Hut to the top of the pass requires 3 to 6 hours depending on the weather, snow conditions, and fitness of your party.

Follow the track from the hut up a gentle slope for a short way north. Erosion now prevents any crossing of the avalanche gully directly to the north of the hut. Within 5 minutes you turn west and, following the orange standard poles, climb a steep, loose scree slope. From the top point, the track now descends a cabled section between two large boulders into a gully below. You are now high above the loose moraine. Continue northward over the rocks and a small scree field and then over a small ridge. Descend the ridge and cross the second scree field; the next ridge is the actual Copland ridge. Look for cairns and a faint trail. From here the Hooker Hut is still in view, far below you and across the tremendous gully. Climbers coming from the west should take care in this area. In the late afternoon visibility can be poor and the tendency is to lose too much elevation on the Copland ridge.

As you ascend the ridge over loose rock, the trail fades occasionally. The rock is easily broken, so beware of loose foot and hand holds so as not to dislodge rocks on to climbers below. Large parties may wish to use helmets. You will need both hands to pull yourself up over the rocks as you quickly gain elevation through some exposed sections. Early in the year if the snow level is low, belays or crampons may be required. You will be able to see Fitzgerald Pass, often confused with the Copland Pass. There are rewarding views back to the Hermitage and Lake Pukaki. In several hours after leaving the Hooker Hut, you will arrive at the Copland Emergency Shelter (1830m). This barrel-shaped shelter, equipped with a radio and shovel, is for emergency use only. It's a good place to enjoy a snack before ascending the final 320 metres to the top of the pass.

After preparing your warm clothing and putting on your crampons, walk to the left of the Emergency Shelter and the huge boulder behind it. Continue up the ridge on the extremely steep snow slope bearing to the right of the two larger boulders located

Mt Sefton and Hooker River swingbridge, Copland Track

about three-quarters of the way up the slope. You will want to zig-zag up the slope, not going too far to the right, since it is steeper here. Late in the season, be aware of icy conditions and of crevasses that may form just below the crest of the pass on the upper left of the slope. Take special care and belay those who are unsteady, as there is no safe run-out, and a misstep could be fatal.

The view to the "top of New Zealand" is breathtaking. The west face of Mt Cook is almost upon you, and you can see south down the Tasman Valley to Lake Pukaki, and if you are lucky, the West Coast will be clear.

From the top of the pass, it's about 4 hours to Douglas Rock hut. To cross the pass, head towards the ridge directly in front of you to the third rock notch from the left, wriggle through the rocks to the pass and cross over. If necessary, use a belay to descend a steep rock chute 50 metres below to the permanent snow and scree field. Next, head down the open snow and rock fields about 1 hour to find the cairn marked track at about 1400 metres, where the zig-zag descent to the floor of the Copland Valley begins. As you pick up the trail, make sure you stay to the left of the creek and waterfall and follow the switchbacks to the head of the Copland Valley. The immense valley below you is a spectacular sight. The straightforward track crosses avalanche gullies and several streams, which may be high early in the year. The gullies may be snow covered, but snow poles, some flattened from the winter snows, mark the way across them. Look for trail markers or poles on the opposite side of the gullies if the marker poles have been dislodged by the winter snows. At all times you remain on the true left and above the Copland River. Kea may greet you as you pause for lunch. Just after entering the bush, the Douglas Rock Hut (sleeps 12/stove/radio) will be a welcome sight.

DOUGLAS ROCK (700m) to WELCOME FLAT (425m)
3.30 hours, 7km

Elevation:	Moderate, parts almost level
Terrain:	Bush, riparian
Special Features:	Hot pools, mountain views

This short day may be considered by many to be a well deserved rest. At the hut, the route changes back to a well-worn track. You will come in 5 minutes to the Tekano Creek footbridge, cross a spur, but will at all times be following above the Copland River. For the first hour after leaving the hut, you need to maneuver around, up and over large tree roots, and climb up and down into stream beds. This may be tiresome after the previous day's crossing. From openings through the bush, there are good views back to the head of the Copland Valley. Finally, after emerging from the bush and just after fording Scott Creek, which may be difficult to cross after a heavy rain, you emerge into the open grassland of Welcome Flat. One and a quarter hours from the next hut, you may find the flats a good place for a break. The track meanders in and out of the grassland and river bed. A swingbridge will take you finally to the true right of the river and 100 metres east to the new spacious Welcome Flat Hut built in 1987 (sleeps 36/rock bivouac sleeps 10/stove/radio/summer warden). You'll find that many of the trampers in the hut have come from the western road end at SH 6 to soak in the hot pools.

It is here that you will no doubt spend the rest of the day testing the three hot pools located behind the hut, each a different temperature. The first is tepid, the second resembles a hot bath, and the third approaches scalding. Submerge yourself (except your head for fear of meningitis) and you'll have not a care in the world for the rest of the day. Even cold rain cannot spoil this highlight of the trip! The Sierra range looms above, and Mt Sefton commands the head of the valley.

WELCOME FLAT (425m) to STATE HIGHWAY 6 at
KARANGARUA RIVER (50m)
5.30 hours, 17km

Elevation:	Gradual
Terrain:	Bush, riparian

The track soon leaves the memories of the mountains behind as it begins with a short 1 kilometre climb through bush to the highest point for the day at Shiels Creek. Five minutes after the creek is a rock bivouac, located 5 minutes from the trail. The track then winds $1^1/_2$ kilometres slowly downhill to Open Creek, where there is a flood bridge and 2 kilometres further along crosses another bridge over Palaver Creek. You'll then pass the area of the great slip of 1982, where you may have to pick your way over the rock and debris. Continue to descend to Architect Creek, a 300-metre drop from Welcome Flat. There is a nice tent site about 10 minutes along. Thirty minutes farther there is good camping at Pick and Shovel Flat. The track moves in and out of the river bed to the bush in this section. Continue along the track to McPhee Creek and another bridge and, after another 2 kilometres, to a bridge over an unnamed stream. Now, as the track leaves the river to cross several terraces and follows an old bridle track, progress becomes easier. It then crosses a junction to a side track for a view of the Karangarua River. Back in the dense forest for 2 kilometres the track breaks out again to the river flat, where poles mark the way. If it is too difficult to cross the river, you may have to follow the high water route in this section. The Karangarua River road bridge at SH 6 finally comes into view, far in the distance. Back into the forest for a short time, the track emerges at Rough Creek. Ford the creek at the marker or, if it is in flood, use the flood bridge a full 30 minutes upstream. It's 200 metres to the car park and an intentions book. There is camping here, but the sandflies are numerous. Don't forget to sign out here or at Westland National Park Visitor Centre in Fox where you may pay your hut fees. Much time and energy has been lost on unnecessary searches for trampers who fail to sign out.

GUIDING SERVICES

Alpine Guides, located next to the post office and general store in Mount Cook Village, offers expert guiding throughout Mount Cook and Westland National Parks. To cross the Copland Pass, the guide is normally hired for a period of $1^1/_2$ days with a maximum of three per party. You will be taken over the Copland Pass to the top of the zig-zag on the western side. The guide will then return over the pass to Mount Cook and carry back with him any gear, such as ice axe or crampons, you may have borrowed.

Guiding services are also available through Alpine Guides in Fox Glacier. Since they strongly recommend the east to west crossing as well, a trans-alpine flight from Fox to Mount Cook Village starts your trip. Though undoubtedly an outstanding addition to your holiday, flights are often delayed or cancelled because of poor weather. A longer spell of good weather is thus needed for a successful crossing.

CONTACTS:

Department of Conservation:

Mount Cook National Park Headquarters, PO Box 5, Mount Cook   0-3-435 1819
Westland National Park Visitor Centre, P.O. Box 9, Fox Glacier
0-3-751 0807

(Visitor Information *(i)*)

Alpine Guides (Mount Cook) Ltd, PO Box 20, Mount Cook
0-3-435 1834
Alpine Guides (Westland) Ltd, PO BOX 38, Fox Glacier
0-3-751 0825

CHAPTER 13: **SOUTH ISLAND, SOUTH: MT ASPIRING NATIONAL PARK AND WAKATIPU STATE FOREST**

ROUTEBURN TRACK/GREENSTONE-CAPLES TRACK/REES-DART TRACK

*There are no words that can tell of the hidden spirit
of the wilderness, that can reveal its mystery,
its melancholy and its charm.*

Theodore Roosevelt

Some of New Zealand's best-known walking tracks wind through the region of Mount Aspiring National Park, the official end of the Southern Alps. The centrepiece of this national park is the majestic Mt Aspiring (3027m) that gives the park its name. Stretching from the Haast River in the north to the Humboldt Mountains in the south, the park shares a boundary with Fiordland National Park, where it meets the Hollyford Valley. Many peaks of its peaks exceed 2700 metres and along with its 100 plus glaciers and miles of open river valleys, the park offer endless opportunities for trampers to explore rugged remote terrain.

Two well known walking tracks, the Routeburn and the Rees-Dart, lie within a small area of the park north of Queenstown, near Glenorchy. A third, the Greenstone-Caples, is located in Wakatipu State Forest, southwest of the Routeburn Track. The spectacular views, waterfalls, and alpine terrain of the Routeburn Track, considered by some to be more beautiful than the Milford Track, draws walkers from all over the world. The Greenstone Track, known for its trout fishing, and the Caples Track, which climbs to a sub-alpine basin with outstanding views of the peaks above the Hollyford Valley, share common entry and exit points and connect to the Routeburn Track at Lake Howden. Though less crowded than the Routeburn, they can still be busy during the summer. The Rees-Dart Track, more demanding than either the Routeburn or Greenstone-Caples, follows two wide river valleys of its own and crosses an alpine pass. Splendid views of surrounding mountain ranges and a opportunity for a day trip to the Dart Glacier highlight the trip. The Cascade Saddle Route from the Aspiring Hut in the West Matukituki Valley climbs a difficult 1500 metres to the Cascade Saddle and joins the Rees-Dart Track at the Dart Hut.

WEATHER

As a result of low pressure systems moving in from the Tasman Sea, weather in this area is variable. High amounts of precipitation are common on the western side of the mountains. While annual rainfall in Fiordland, just to the west, is 7000 millimetres, but a bit further east, at Lake Howden, the Routeburn, and the Dart Valley, that figure drops to 5000 millimetres. The drier Rees and Greenstone Valleys record only 1000 millimetres per year. Autumn and spring bring the most unsettled weather. Fine periods of weather can often mark the winter and the months of February and March. Snow covers the higher elevations in winter, so that only the Greenstone Valley remains open all year to trampers.

On the Routeburn track, the exposed section over Harris Pass lies vulnerable to cold winds and driving rain, and there have been deaths from hypothermia on this section. It is wise to plan for an extra day in case of poor weather and better your chances of enjoying the fine views. On the Rees-Dart, you should have good visibility for the crossing of the Rees Saddle.

BASE

Queenstown, a bustling tourist centre on the shores of Lake Wakatipu, boasts a lovely setting beneath the Remarkables mountain range. Choice of accommodation is wide, from luxury hotels, motels, bed and breakfasts, to hostels and backpacker's accommodation. Shops provide almost everything one could want in the way of equipment and supplies. Advertised as the "adventure capital of New Zealand", Queenstown sells thrills from jet boat rides, to parapenting, to bungy-jumping.

A tiny town, Glenorchy, located on the route from Queenstown to all three tracks, has a small store, motor camp, hotel, cafes, and a ranger station. Glenorchy Holiday Park provides transport service from Queenstown to all three tracks.

Several flights a day serve Queenstown from Christchurch on Ansett Airlines, and Mount Cook Airlines connects from Christchurch, Mount Cook, Te Anau, and Dunedin. Both InterCity and Mount Cook Landline have bus connections from Christchurch, Mount Cook, Te Anau, Dunedin, Invercargill and Wanaka. InterCity provides daily service to/from the Glaciers on the West Coast. Backpacker's transport serves Queenstown from the Glaciers and Christchurch. For information on these services, check at a Visitor Information Network *(i)*, or directly with the bus company.

ROUTEBURN TRACK

The Routeburn Track is one of the best known and finest walks in New Zealand. This spectacular subalpine crossing extends between Mount Aspiring National Park from the Routeburn Valley across the Harris Saddle and Humboldt Mountains into Fiordland National Park. It ends at the Divide on the Te Anau - Milford Highway. Much of the track is above timberline, and the section between Lake Mackenzie Hut and Routeburn Falls over Harris Saddle (1237m) offers unparalleled views.

HISTORY

To the early inhabitants of this land, the Maori, and to the early European explorers, the Routeburn Valley was a vital link between Lake Wakatipu and the Hollyford Valley. A route from Queenstown to the West Coast was first proposed in 1863, but the job was felt to be too difficult to be attempted. In 1870 a track which was to connect to the Hollyford Valley was begun over Harris Saddle but this too was abandoned for lack of funds. In the late 1890s tourists were first taken via the Routeburn Flats by horseback and then they would climb up to Harris Saddle. The current track connected with the earlier abandoned track. The track finally reached Lake Howden by the end of World War I and was completed to the Divide when the Milford Road was finally cut in the 1930s.

TRACK ACCESS

The track can be walked in either direction: from east to west using Queenstown as a base, or from west to east with Queenstown or Te Anau as headquarters. If travelling from west to east, several buses a day going to Milford from Queenstown and Te Anau on Mount Cookline and InterCity stop at the Divide. Kiwi Backpacker and Kiwi Discovery also offer bus transportation from Queenstown and Te Anau. All buses continue on to the Divide, Marian Corner and Milford. If you wish to view the Milford Sound, continue on to Milford, take the boat tour, and catch the afternoon bus back to Te Anau, getting off at the Divide. From there you can walk to the Lake Howden Hut for the night. To find out about all the various transport options available, visit the Information and Track Centre in Queenstown.

Those travelling in the east-to-west direction and walking the Routeburn track only, may take a bus from Queenstown to the Routeburn Shelter in the morning, and on finishing the track at the Divide, catch the afternoon bus returning to Te Anau. Bus reservations in both directions are recommended, especially in high season.

THE TRACK

The 39 kilometre easy track is appropriate for any reasonably fit tramper and families with hiking experience. The track is well-maintained, nicely graded, and its huts are clean and comfortable. The track may be walked in either direction. However, trampers walking from west to east (the "Divide" to Routeburn Flats) have a choice of using either the Flats or Falls hut on the last night, an advantage during the busy season.

The Routeburn is also one of the most heavily travelled tracks,

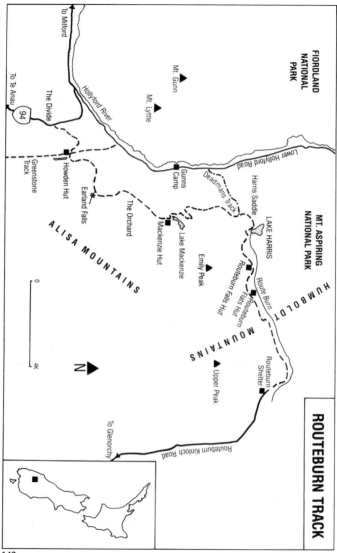

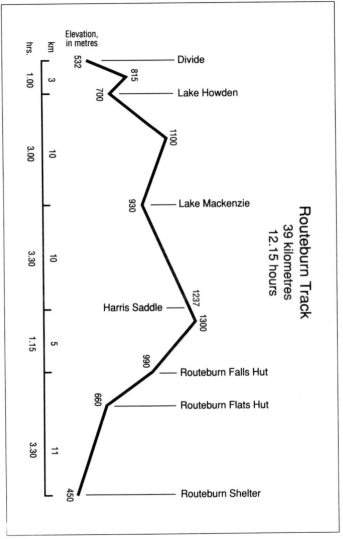

Elevation, in metres

Routeburn Track
39 kilometres
12.15 hours

532 — Divide
815
700 — Lake Howden
1100
930 — Lake Mackenzie
1237
Harris Saddle — 1300
990 — Routeburn Falls Hut
660 — Routeburn Flats Hut
450 — Routeburn Shelter

km: 3, 10, 10, 5, 11
hrs: 1.00, 3.00, 3.30, 1.15, 3.30

visited each year by some 9000 trampers from all parts of the world. If you want solitude, seek another track. In my view, though, what you lose in solitude, you more than make up for in lively exchanges with people from far places. The varied and spectacular scenery make for an exciting trip and it's one of my favourite tramps.

THE DIVIDE (532m) to LAKE HOWDEN (700m)
1.00 hours, 3km

Terrain:	Bush
Elevation:	Moderate

The bus will drop you off at the Divide, the lowest east-west crossing of the Southern Alps, where there is a public restroom and shelter. From that point the track climbs gradually through thick forest and in about 30 minutes reaches the turn off to Key Summit (815m). A side trip to Key Summit (919m) is well worth the effort in fine weather (1 hour return). If you choose this side trip, you shortly leave the heavy bush and travel up through an area of open territory. In about 20 minutes, you reach an area of tarns and bogs. Unusual plants, such as orchids, sundew, bogpine, proliferate amid the low-growing mountain beech. Views of the Darran mountains and Lake Marian are spectacular. An extra 30 minutes along the ridgeline opens up views of the Greenstone and Eglinton Valleys. It is advisable to stay on the trail in this fragile alpine area.

Returning to the main trail, you have another 15 minutes of gradual downhill through thick beech before you arrive at the nicely designed Lake Howden Hut (sleeps 28/gas/stove/summer warden) which has a comfortable mezzanine sleeping area. If you're tall, duck your head when stepping onto the porch. The hut sits at the junction of the Routeburn and Greenstone tracks, from where the Greenstone Track heads south to Lake McKellar. Another trail branches north down Pass Creek to the Lower Hollyford Road. Camping is allowed only at the far end of Lake Howden about 20 minutes from the hut, a short way south on the Greenstone Track.

LAKE HOWDEN (700m) to LAKE MACKENZIE (930m)
3.00 hours, 10km

Terrain:	Bush, riparian
Elevation:	Moderate; parts steep
Special Features:	Mountain views; valley views, waterfall

The track rises moderately, at first in bush. In about an hour the thick growth breaks open affording a fine view of Lake McKerrow, the lower Hollyford, and Gunns Camp. After a gain of 400 metres and $1^1/_2$ hours, the track passes over rocks at the base of thundering Earland Falls (1100m), which can be heard from half a kilometre away. If the falls are in flood, you may use the emergency bridge just downstream. The trail continues on the edge of the bush but breaks out frequently for fine views of the Hollyford Valley and Darran Mountains. Within another 30 minutes you descend gradually to the "Orchard", a clearing in the bush with ribbonwood trees that resemble fruit trees. Continuing high on the margin of the bush through mountain beech, the trail crosses Roaring Creek, and then descends steeply through thick growth to a grass clearing past a private hut owned by Routeburn Walk Ltd to Lake Mackenzie. At the far end, Emily Peak (1820m) dominates, and on a fine day its reflections may be seen in the lake. The popular Lake Mackenzie Hut (sleeps 56/gas/summer warden) has recently been enlarged to accommodate the large numbers of trampers who congregate here. A camping area with eight sites, an outhouse, and a sheltered area for cooking, can be found just before the Mackenzie Hut.

LAKE MACKENZIE (930m) to ROUTEBURN FALLS HUT (990m) via HARRIS SADDLE (1237m)
4.45 hours, 15km

Terrain:	Bush, grassland
Elevation:	Steep, parts gradual
Special Features:	Mountain views, mountain pass, waterfall

Crossing below Lake Mackenzie on a trail strewn with boulders, follow the sharp well formed zigzag rise of 300 metres, initially through bush. The trees draped with moss give evidence of the high rainfall in this area. Leaving the bush, you are afforded striking views of Emily Peak with clouds often swirling in and about its top after a heavy rain. The trail continues to climb until you round Ocean Peak Corner and head north. For the next 2 hours, the track sidles the Hollyford Face well above the bushline. On a fine day this section of the track makes the Routeburn one of the most spectacular walks in New Zealand. Unparalleled views of the Darran Mountains with towering Mt Christina and Mt Tutoko fill the skyline as you walk above the Hollyford Valley. You can follow the valleys route to Lake McKerrow and Martins Bay. Extra care should be taken on this section during foul weather as it is exposed to high winds and freezing temperatures. Within 30 minutes after beginning the traverse a footbridge leads you over Potters Creek, and within 10 minutes on your left and below the track is a huge rock bivouac that in an emergency can be used by up to four people. Within one hour more, you cross the lateral Deadmans Track, an extremely steep trail to the Hollyford Valley (4-5 hours). The trail then clings to the side of the ridge and approaches its low point. You then ascend some stairs (Stairway to Heaven) to a knob above Harris Saddle (1237m). The track weaves through some tarns past the turn-off to Conical Hill. In clear weather, a trip to Conical Hill (1 hour return and an additional 240 metres of ascent) is worthwhile for its 360-degree view of the Darran Mountains and the Hollyford Valley. Near the top of the saddle, a popular lunch spot, stands a shelter meant for emergency purposes only.

From the saddle the track climbs for 15 minutes on rocky bluffs above the spectacular blue Lake Harris to its true high point (1300m). The trail slowly drops 1 hour through a lovely sub-alpine basin through tussocks and tiny streams to Routeburn Falls Hut (sleeps 30/gas/stove/summer warden). In clear weather there are fine views towards Routeburn Flats and tomorrow's walk. This hut, even though recently enlarged, can be crowded, and the veranda filled with an overflow of trampers. Trampers arriving at the hut early in the day have the option of dropping down to the Routeburn

Flats Hut. If the hut is overcrowded, beds may be available nevertheless at the Flats Hut. The resident kea population may greet you on your arrival, or awaken you in the morning by sliding down the hut's tin roof shrieking their familiar call: "kkkk-eeee-aaaa!" The upper private hut is owned by Routeburn Walk Ltd.

Kea at Routeburn Falls Hut, Routeburn Track

ROUTEBURN FALLS (990m) to ROUTEBURN FLATS (660m)
1.00 hours, 3km

Terrain: Bush, riparian
Elevation: Steep

Continue into the verdant bush and begin the steep descent for 3 kilometres to Routeburn Flats Hut (20 bunks/gas/stove/summer warden), which has recently been upgraded to encourage more trampers. The hut is a 5-minute walk from the track. There are two bunk rooms, a separate kitchen, and a central lounge with a wood stove. From the hut you may enjoy fine views across the river to Mt Somnus and the Humboldt Mountains. A pleasant camping spot lies 200 metres past the hut in the grass covered flats on the Route Burn.

ROUTEBURN FLATS (660m) to ROUTEBURN SHELTER (450m)
2.30 hours, 8km

Terrain: Bush, riparian
Elevation: Almost level
Special Features: Mountain views

From the hut follow the trail across the grassy flats to the footbridge and cross the Route Burn to the true left of the river. There is an emergency track in the bush around the flats. Following the Route Burn gorge, the track enters the bush, crossing a number of small fast streams. All major streams are bridged. Moving high above the river, Bridal Veil and Sugar Loaf streams are crossed, the trail drops slowly on the north side of the river to a footbridge downstream from the shelter. The shelter is for day use only. You can catch the bus from here to Glenorchy and Queenstown.

CAMPING

Camping is allowed within 500 metres of the Routeburn Track only in designated campsites at Lake Mackenzie and at Routeburn Flats, or 20 minutes south of Lake Howden. There is a small charge for use of the campsites at Lake Mackenzie; the others may be used without charge.

GUIDED TOURS

Between November and April, Routeburn Walk Ltd offers a three-day two-night guided trek of the Routeburn Track with a maximum of twenty people. The walk includes guiding, as well as private lodging, meals and bedding at Lake Mackenzie and Routeburn Falls. Walkers must carry their own clothing, but packs and wet-weather gear are loaned when needed. The Routeburn Walk operates in one direction only from the "Divide" to the Route Burn, as described here. This can be combined with the Greenstone Valley Walk for "The Grand Traverse". (See description of the Greenstone-Caples.)

GREENSTONE-CAPLES TRACK

The Greenstone and the Caples Tracks together make a circular 69-kilometre route, connecting at entry and exit points. The Greenstone Track joins up with the Routeburn Track at Lake Howden at the western end, and meets the Caples Track 20 minutes from the Greenstone car park in the east. Both tracks take two days each; if walked together, the route requires four days.

HISTORY

The area was first explored by Maori hunters looking for the giant moa bird. As early as 1500 AD, the Maori obtained greenstone from the Wakatipu field in the Dart Valley and transported it to the West Coast. At that time, greenstone was used for tools and weapons; today it is popular for jewelry. Greenstone seeking expeditions were thought to continue until the 1850s, when the Europeans first explored the region.

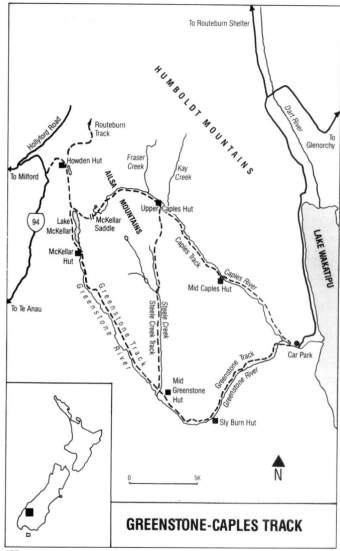

GREENSTONE-CAPLES TRACK

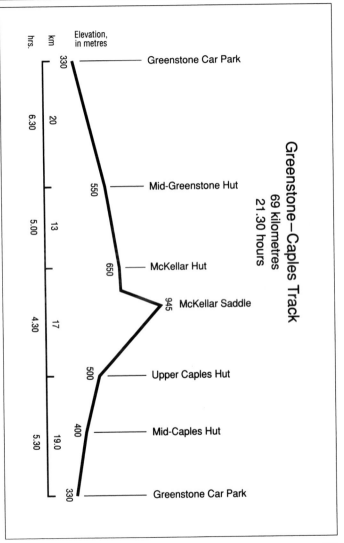

Greenstone–Caples Track
69 kilometres
21.30 hours

Elevation, in metres	Location
330	Greenstone Car Park
550	Mid-Greenstone Hut
650	McKellar Hut
945	McKellar Saddle
500	Upper Caples Hut
400	Mid-Caples Hut
330	Greenstone Car Park

Greenstone Valley and Lake McKellar, Greenstone Track

It was in 1861 that David McKellar and George Gunn arrived looking for grazing lands near Lake Howden. In 1863, Patrick Caples, a goldminer, made an expedition into the area, discovered the Harris Saddle, and descended into the Hollyford Valley. Caples apparently ventured up the Hollyford Valley out to the Tasman Sea. He returned home through the valley that now bears his name.

In 1881 a rough track was cut through the valley to connect with a settlement at Martins Bay. The steamship Earnslaw first departed from Queenstown to Elfin Bay in 1912 to bring trampers to walk up the Greenstone Valley. Today an unsealed road connects Glenorchy with Kinloch and the Routeburn Shelter. The opening of the Dart River Bridge in 1974 vastly improved access to these tracks, although today, weather permitting, trampers still enjoy a boat trip across Lake Wakatipu from Glenorchy to the start of the Greenstone-Caples Tracks.

TRACK ACCESS

InterCity, Mount Cook Landline, Kiwi Backpackers and Kiwi Experience have frequent bus service from Queenstown and Te Anau to the Divide and Milford. To reach the western junction of the Greenstone and Caples Tracks, walk 3 kilometres on the Routeburn Track to the Lake Howden Hut (28 bunks/gas/ stove/summer warden). It's another 3.5 kilometres south along the Greenstone Track to Lake McKellar to the junction of the two tracks. If you are coming from the east, Glenorchy Holiday Park provides a bus from Queenstown to Glenorchy, and a boat across Lake Wakatipu to the Greenstone car park. Twenty minutes up the trail through beech forest, and you reach the eastern junction of the Greenstone and Caples Track.

GREENSTONE TRACK

The 36.5 kilometre Greenstone Track, measured from the eastern car park on Lake Wakatipu to the northern end of Lake McKellar, travels along the Greenstone River Valley, which is noted for its emerald pools, fine fishing, and wide open river valleys. Gradual elevation gains and losses, bridged river crossings, and well-manicured trails earn the trip an easy classification. The track may

153

Greenstone Valley, Greenstone Track

be walked in either direction

GREENSTONE CAR PARK (EAST) (330m) to MID-GREENSTONE HUT (550m)
6.30 hours, 20km

Terrain:	Bush, forest, riparian
Elevation:	Moderate
Special Features:	Mountain views

From the Greenstone-Caples car park, follow the track uphill 20 minutes to the junction of the Greenstone-Caples Track. Take the left fork to the first swingbridge (turn right if going to the Caples) over a huge chasm to the southern side of the Greenstone River. Just across the bridge the track joins a wide cattle trail and comes to a lovely view of the confluence of the Greenstone-Caples Rivers. Twenty minutes over grassy flats brings you to another swingbridge which takes you to the northern side and true left of the Greenstone

154

River. Look for magnificent swimming and fishing pools in this area. A good track continues gradually through the Greenstone Gorge with the river rushing below. In 2 hours, you'll pass a side track heading east to Elfin Bay and Lake Wakatipu. Ten minutes more at hilly Slip Flat you leave the bush for a short period. In 1 hour you'll pass a side track to Sly Burn Hut (sleeps 10/stove) and a good view into a river gorge. Back on the main track, you'll emerge quickly out into the open flat Greenstone Valley. On a fine day, Mt Christina rises over the Livingstone Mountains at the head of the valley. It's another hour along the grasslands to the Mid-Greenstone Hut (12 bunks/stove/summer warden) and another 15 minutes along for guided walkers to Steele Creek Lodge.

MID-GREENSTONE HUT (550m) to McKELLAR HUT (650m)
5.00 hours, 13km

Terrain:	Bush, forest, riparian
Elevation:	Gradual
Special Features:	Mountain views

Twenty minutes after you leave the hut, just after the swingbridge, the difficult Steele Creek Track heads north and crosses the Ailsa mountains to the Upper Caples Hut (10 hours). In 1 kilometre, take a short detour to the mid-Greenstone Gorge with the river cutting through the valley's rocky walls. After the mid-Greenstone Gorge you can ford the river and walk up the western side of the valley. This offers the least boggy walk for those wanting dry feet as well as a tramp out in the open. The track continues on the true left of the river gradually advancing up the bush-laden valley, only occasionally breaking out of the bush to present a view of the mountains on both sides. Fishing is reported to be excellent in this area. The last 15 minutes you pass into heavy bush and cross a swingbridge to McKellar Hut (20 bunks/stove/summer warden) not far from the southern edge of Lake McKellar. Guided walkers will find their hut 5 minutes along the route. Just below the outlet to the lake a wooden bridge crosses to the eastern side and leads on a track to a plunging waterfall.

McKELLAR HUT (650m) to LAKE HOWDEN HUT (700m)
2.00 hours, 7km

Terrain: Bush, riparian
Elevation: Almost level
Special Features: Mountain views

From behind the McKellar hut, follow the track in bush along the western shores of Lake McKellar. If you are continuing on to Lake Howden, it's 3.5 kilometres to the junction of the Greenstone-Caples Tracks in an open grassy clearing at the northern edge of Lake McKellar. If you are heading on to the Caples Track, turn right here at the track sign to begin the climb up the McKellar Saddle. It's 3¹/₂ hours from here to the Upper Caples Hut.

If you are continuing on to the Divide, Lake Howden or the Routeburn Track, the Greenstone Track crosses the low Greenstone Saddle in bush, and in 30 minutes and 2.5 kilometres reaches the southern end of Lake Howden, where there is good camping. Follow the track at the edge of the lake 1 kilometre and 20 minutes to its northern end at the Howden Hut. See notes under the Routeburn Track description for details of the 3 kilometre section going to the Divide at the Te Anau - Milford Road.

CAPLES TRACK
The Caples Track, completing a loop with the Greenstone Track, extends 32.5 kilometres from the north end of Lake McKellar to the Greenstone car park. A smaller and more compact valley than the neighbouring Greenstone, the Caples climbs a scenic, subalpine pass with beautiful views into Fiordland National Park. The track may be walked in either direction, although climbing up the slippery pass raises its designation to moderate. The lower sections nearer to the Greenstone have good trout fishing.

GREENSTONE-CAPLES TRACK JUNCTION (WEST) (660m) to
UPPER CAPLES HUT (500m) via McKELLAR SADDLE (945m)
3.30 hours, 13.5km

Terrain:	Bush, riparian
Elevation:	Extremely steep, parts steep
Special Features:	Mountain views

Cross the boggy area just north of Lake McKellar and head south
along the lake's eastern shore in the heavy bush. The 400 metre
1½ hour ascent to McKellar Saddle (945m) is a stiff one. Take care
not to slip on the tree roots and hold onto branches for support. You
come out of the bush onto a tarn speckled saddle and a Fiordland
National Park signpost. To the west and south you get outstanding
views of the peaks of Fiordland National Park, framed by the
saddle's lone tree. As you cross the one kilometre pass, take care not
to hurt the fragile alpine environment. There are good views ahead
to the Humboldt Mountains and Mt Bonpland (2348m). Crossing
the saddle, you come upon orange standards which mark the 450
metre descent into the bush. In 1 hour you will cross to the true left
of the Caples River. Continuing your descent another 150 metres,
you cross in 30 minutes to the true right of the Caples River. The
tree's extensive root system intertwines with the track. About 3
hours from the pass, you'll come to an open clearing and the Upper
Caples Hut (20 bunks/stove/summer warden). Difficult side tracks
up Fraser and Kay Creeks begin on the other side of the bridge.

UPPER CAPLES HUT (500m) to MID CAPLES HUT (400m)
2.30 hours 9km

Terrain:	Bush, riparian
Elevation:	Almost level

Fifteen minutes after you leave the hut, you'll come across the turn
off to Upper Caples-Steele Creek Track, a high-level difficult route
to the mid-Greenstone Valley. Leaving the short bush section, you

follow on the true right of the river through open grassland and some private property with protective fences. The track ascends briefly through a beech forest but quickly descends again to the grassland. Pleasant open-valley walking brings you to the Mid-Caples Hut (12 bunks/stove/summer warden) located in a clearing on a shelf above the river.

MID-CAPLES HUT (400m) to GREENSTONE CAR PARK (330m)
3.00 hours, 10km

Terrain:	Bush, riparian
Elevation:	Almost level

From the Mid-Caples Hut, you immediately cross a footbridge high above a gorge in the Caples River. It's a peaceful relaxing walk down the valley, where the trail avoids the open grazing land and stays in beech forest. The old Birchdale homestead is across the river. When you come to the signposted junction to the Greenstone Track, it's another 20 minutes to the car park.

CAMPING

The open grazing land in both the Greenstone and Caples Valley is leased. If you wish to camp, please do so on the bush edge.

GUIDED TOURS

Routeburn Walk Ltd offers a six day combined Routeburn-Greenstone Walk, the "Grand Traverse", or a three day Greenstone Walk. Pleasant, well-equipped huts with bunk rooms, showers, and large common areas are located at Steele Creek and Lake McKellar in the Greenstone Valley and on the Routeburn at Lake Mackenzie and Routeburn Falls. You carry only your own gear; food is provided for you. Groups are limited to twenty clients with one guide per seven clients.

REES-DART TRACK

This strenuous four to five day 76.5 kilometre track links the magnificent Rees and Dart Valleys with a variety of bush and open country highlighted by magnificent mountain views. The trip may be walked in either direction, although it's a more gradual ascent to the Rees Saddle from the Rees Valley. More difficult than the neighbouring Routeburn, or Greenstone-Caples, the track requires previous tramping experience.

TRACK ACCESS

If you have your own car, drive the 50 kilometres on unsealed road from Queenstown to Glenorchy, and leave your car at the Glenorchy Holiday Park. From here pick up the once daily morning bus to Muddy Creek. Upon finishing the track at Paradise catch the mid-afternoon bus back to Glenorchy. Glenorchy Holiday Park has two buses a day into/from Queenstown. The morning bus connects with the shuttle to Muddy Creek at the start of the Rees Valley. Cost of the evening bus includes a night at the holiday park and transportation to the track the next morning.

REES VALLEY ROAD END (457m) to
TWENTY-FIVE MILE HUT (533m)
2.00 hours, 6.5km

Elevation:	Almost level
Terrain:	Grassland
Special Features:	Mountain views; river crossings

From the Muddy Creek car park in the lower Rees Valley, the track follows an old vehicle road through private land. In early season, you may have to ford Bridges or Arthurs Creek, where there is a private hut. You continue up the grassy flats on the true left of the Rees River. The old Twenty-Five Mile Hut (sleeps 8) can be seen

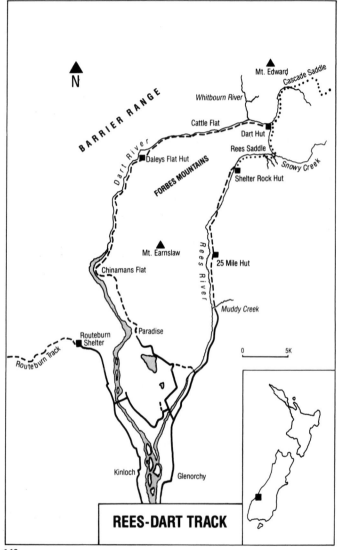

REES-DART TRACK

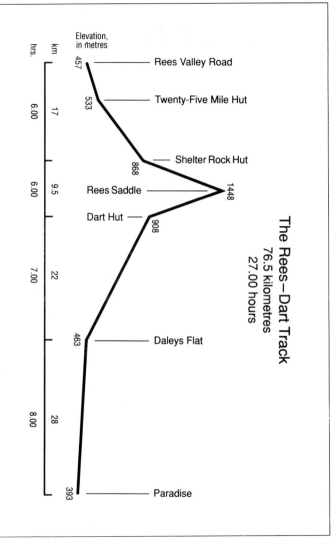

Elevation, in metres

hrs. / km

457 — Rees Valley Road

533 — Twenty-Five Mile Hut

6.00 / 17

868 — Shelter Rock Hut

6.00 / 9.5

Rees Saddle — 1448

Dart Hut — 908

7.00 / 22

The Rees–Dart Track
76.5 kilometres
27.00 hours

463 — Daleys Flat

8.00 / 28

393 — Paradise

161

near the bush edge in a clump of trees, 60 metres above the valley floor. The hut may be difficult to locate if coming from the north, but Lennox Falls is located just northwest of the hut on the opposite side of the river. Clear weather affords good views of Mt Earnslaw.

TWENTY FIVE MILE HUT (533m) to SHELTER ROCK HUT (868m)
4.00 hours, 10.5km

Elevation:	Moderate, parts steep
Terrain:	Bush, grassland, riparian
Special Features:	Mountain views

Past the hut, continue up the valley in open country on the river's true left. The track fades, and can be easily lost as you wander through the flats. In early season, the track may be quite boggy, and you will want to cross on higher ground over some steep and slippery grassy outcroppings, a bit away from the river. Further along, if you lose the track, simply walk straight up the valley along the flats or follow the orange and white marker poles. In 1¹/₂ hours, you enter the bush at a Mount Aspiring National Park Boundary sign. Ten minutes from here you cross to the river's true right on a swingbridge, and in 1 hour emerge from the bush at Clark Slip. The track continues through bush again, and with convenient footbridges, this uphill section is uncomplicated. You pass the old Shelter Rock Hut site, then sidle through some steep side gullies, which may have snow in early season, and through an old avalanche area. About 4 hours from the Twenty-Five Mile Hut and 30 minutes from the old hut site, you reach Shelter Rock Hut (sleeps 10/stove), across a swingbridge on the river's true left.

SHELTER ROCK HUT (868m) to DART HUT (908m)
via REES SADDLE (1448m)
6.00 hours, 9.5km

Elevation:	Steep; parts extremely steep
Terrain:	Grassland; riparian
Special Features:	Mountain views; glacier views; mountain pass

You should have good visibility for the crossing of the Rees Saddle. From Shelter Rock Hut on the true left of the Rees River, climb up to the end of the valley on a series of shelves through tussocks and through some vicious sharp spaniard grass. Marked by cairns and orange standards, the route leads along a stream bed to the Rees Saddle, the obvious low point to the northeast. In a little over 2 hours, you'll reach the base of a short, steep 100-metre scramble up to the Rees Saddle. Before you reach the saddle, the faint track follows close to the base of a rock wall, but this may be snow covered late into the season. Though views are limited from the saddle, it's a fine place for a rest or lunch.

Descending from the saddle, follow the rutted trail and snow standards high above Snowy Creek. As you move down the valley, the views open up to the views of the Hesse and Marshall Glacier and icefalls of Mt Edward. After 1 hour, you'll cross to the true right of the river on a swingbridge. This collapsible bridge crosses the Snowy from mid-November to the end of April. Outside of these months, you'll have to use the walkwire or ford the

Mt Cook lily, Rees-Dart Track

163

river. Early in the season, waterfalls plunge into Snowy Creek and fields of Mount Cook lilies bloom here. Follow the extremely steep, deeply cut track as the Dart Hut becomes visible below. There are campsites before crossing on a swingbridge to the Dart Hut (sleeps 20/stove/gas/summer warden). From here, take advantage of splendid day trips to the Dart Glacier, and for the fit, to the Cascade Saddle, where there are fine views of Mt Aspiring. You may wish to visit the Whitbourn Glacier as well.

DART HUT (908m) to DALEYS FLAT HUT (463m)
7.00 hours, 22km

Elevation:	Moderate; parts almost level
Terrain:	Bush, grassland, riparian
Special Features:	Mountain views

From the hut, you immediately enter bush, and in the last few years this section of the track has been rerouted and upgraded. In 20 minutes, however, you'll confront rockier and steeper sections. There are a few views of the Dart River, as you walk above the river's true left. In 45 minutes, you reach the sidetrack to the Whitbourn River, and in another 30 minutes you cross the river leaving the bush only momentarily. About 3 hours after leaving the hut, you cross the seemingly endless 4 kilometres of grassy covered shelves of Cattle Flat. Half way across the flats, a visit to the huge rock bivvy located on the left a few minutes off the trail will break the monotony. Sight of an old airstrip and footbridge crossing the river add some interest to the scenery.

Continuing across Cattle Flat, use the stile to cross a fence and enter the bush once again. In another hour, you drop slowly to the river's edge, breaking out of the bush at the lovely Quinns Flat, and then return again to the bush. In another 30 minutes, you'll be glad to see the Daleys Flat Hut (sleeps 20/stove) in the distance on a shelf above the river.

DALEYS FLAT HUT(463m) to ROAD END at PARADISE (393m)
8.00 hours, 28km

Elevation:	Almost level
Terrain:	Bush, grassland, riparian
Special Features:	Mountain views

A long, rewarding, though not difficult, day awaits you marked by fine views of surrounding peaks. Be sure to leave the hut early, leaving plenty of time to reach the road end to meet transportation to Glenorchy.

The track goes immediately into the bush, and in 15 minutes breaks out onto a flat, but returns right away to the bush. In about an hour, the track crosses Dredge Flat. The remains of the old dredge (c.1900) lie in a hollow immediately opposite when you break out of the bush at the front of the flat. A clump of trees marks the spot. Entering the forest again, the track climbs a 100 metre steep bluff using ladders and steel cables over a rock face. From here, you've a fine view of the Flat and valley. Then, 2 hours from the hut, the track descends to grassy Sandy Flat. Now the track will alternate between forest away from the river and along the river bank. At the unmistakable Chinamans Bluff with its fine mountain views, you climb a bit again. Back at the river level, the track picks up an old vehicle road and in 1¹/₂ hours takes you through the flat grassy lands to the road end at Paradise.

COMBINATION WALKS

This walk can be combined with several others for an unforgettable two to three week tramping holiday. Beginning in Te Anau, walk the Milford Track (four days) and spend the night in Milford, resupplying and touring Milford Sound (one day). Since supplies are limited at Milford, you might consider sending supplies ahead to Milford on either Mount Cook Landline or InterCity bus services. After the tour of the Sound, take a bus to the Divide and walk the 1 hour to the Lake Howden Hut. (See the Routeburn Track description below.) The Greenstone-Caples loop (four days) can be walked from Lake Howden, followed by the Routeburn as described in the text and finishing at the Routeburn Valley Road. The hardy can take the bus to Glenorchy, resupply there, and add on the Dart-Rees track (four to five days), returning to Queenstown at the end of the tramp.

CONTACTS:

Department of Conservation:

Glenorchy Field Centre, PO Box 2, Glenorchy	0-3-442 9937
Cnr. Stanley and Ballarat Street, Queenstown	0-3-442 7933

Visitor Information Network Office (*i*), Clock Tower Centre,

Cnr Shotover and Camp Streets, Queenstown	0-3-442 8238

Information and Track Centre, 37 Shotover St, Queenstown

0-3-442 7028

Kiwi Backpacker, Agents: Information and Track Centre,

37 Shotover, Queenstown	0-3-442 7028
or Air Fiordland, Jailhouse Mall, Te Anau	0-3-249 7505
Kiwi Discovery, Camp Street, Queenstown	0-3-442 7340
Routeburn Walk Ltd, Box 568, Queenstown	0-3-442 8200
Glenorchy Holiday Park, 2 Oban Street, Glenorchy	0-3-442 9939

CHAPTER 14: **SOUTH ISLAND, FAR SOUTH: FIORDLAND NATIONAL PARK**

MILFORD TRACK/KEPLER TRACK/ HOLLYFORD TRACK

Climb the mountains and get their good tidings.
Nature's peace will flow into you as sunshine flows into trees.
The winds will blow their freshness into you, and the storms
their energy, while cares will drop off like autumn leaves.

John Muir

Fiordland, New Zealand's largest National Park, and a part of the South-West New Zealand World Heritage Park, stretches from Martins Bay in the north, to the Tasman Sea in the west, to Preservation Inlet in the south. In the east, it extends to a series of lakes and to the Hollyford and Waiau Rivers, which separate the area from the drier Southland. Heavy rain which creates rich forests, raging rivers and a dense undergrowth of ferns and shrubs has prevented large-scale habitation. On the western edge fourteen fiords, some rising over a kilometre out of the water, indent the rocky coastline. Few visitors to New Zealand miss a visit to Milford Sound by car; the privileged few have the experience of walking through this seemingly impenetrable landscape.

The inaccessibility of this land has protected its birds and wildlife from many of the hazards of civilization. Around Milford Sound the kakapo, a flightless ground parrot, lived in large numbers in the 1800s. With the introduction of European rat and stoat, the numbers decreased remarkably, and none are thought to exist there today. Today the population of less than fifty birds may only be found on predator free offshore islands. Just outside Te Anau, in the Murchison Mountains the takahe, a lovely flightless bird with a midnight blue body and an orange beak, once thought to be extinct, was rediscovered in 1948.

Maori legend claims that Fiordland is the work of the god Tu, who wished to create a land where man would live forever. This distressed the underworld goddess of death, Hinenuitepo who felt the threat of unemployment. Thus as the story goes, she created the sandfly, the namu, to discourage human beings from lingering in the area. These troublesome pesky insects, found in many parts of New Zealand, are notorious among all visitors. The goddess did her work well!

Fiordland is the home of three of New Zealand's best known walking tracks. The world famous Milford Track extends to the northern tip of Lake Te Anau over Mackinnon Pass connecting the Clinton and Arthur Rivers to Milford Sound. The Hollyford Track follows the Hollyford River below the Darran Mountains to Martins Bay on the Tasman Sea. The Kepler Track, New Zealand's newest, runs a circular route through the alpine regions of the Kepler Mountains, adjacent to the small town of Te Anau.

WEATHER

This area of New Zealand has some of the highest rainfall anywhere in the world. Westerlies which blow in from the Tasman Sea are responsible for much of the 7000 millimetres per year that falls in Milford Sound. Heavy rains are thus the norm, and snow is possible even during the summer months. Rain can be especially fierce when crossing the Mackinnon Pass on the Milford Track, and temperatures can fall as much as 15°C in one hour. Water up to one metre deep many have to be forded after heavy rains. Closures of the Milford Track due to high rainfall and flooding may occur anytime of year. Although actual rainfall is lower in the Te Anau area, about 1300 millimetres a year, trampers should be careful of foul weather and high winds on the exposed ridges of the Kepler track, between Luxmore and Iris Burn Huts. Rain and sandflies can be fierce in the Hollyford Valley as well. Be wary of rising rivers. River crossings should be approached with great caution, and, walkwires used if necessary.

BASE

Te Anau, a sleepy little town on the shores of Lake Te Anau, 167 kilometres SW of Queenstown on SH 94, provides several pleasant places to rest up after tramps. It has a hotel, motels, bed-and-breakfast accommodation, and motor camps. Budget accommodation includes a youth hostel on the Milford Road, and a backpacker's lodge. Stores sell a limited range of supplies and sporting equipment.

Accommodation in Milford, 119 kilometres NNE of Te Anau on SH 94, are limited to the hotel, where the guided walkers stay for the night, and budget accommodation, a 20 minute walk down the road from town. There is a pub, a small airport, and not much else. For trampers continuing on to other tracks, opportunity to resupply is limited.

Several buses a day connect Te Anau with Queenstown on Mount Cook Landline, with one bus a day connecting Te Anau with Christchurch and Mount Cook. InterCity serves Te Anau from Queenstown as well, with connections to Invercargill. Kiwi Backpacker and Kiwi Discovery offer bus transportation from Queenstown to Te Anau. All these buses continue on to the Divide and Milford.

Mount Cook Airline has one return flight a day connecting Queenstown with Te Anau. Independent walkers travelling to Te Anau by air will find that the daily Mount Cook airlines flight arrives too late to connect to the Milford Track that same day. Arrangements should be made to arrive at least one day prior to departure. Guided walkers begin their six-day package with a slide show and introductory talk the evening of the first day, the night before the commencement of the actual walk.

MILFORD TRACK

The Milford Track's reputation as "the finest walk in the world" reaches across oceans and lures trampers from the far corners of the world. Trampers are greeted with ghoulish moss laden forests, plunging waterfalls from all directions, playful kea, and a dramatic, if not wet and windy, crossing of Mackinnon Pass. They follow the same route of the early English explorers who for many years searched for an overland passage between Milford Sound and the interior.

For decades after 1903 when the government assumed control of the track, the 53 kilometre trail was open only to guided parties, who stayed at the three Tourist Hotel Corporation (THC) huts. Many complaints about the strict regulations and high costs resulted, finally in 1966, to the granting of access to "freedom walkers". These independent trampers, for a small fraction of the cost of the guided trek, stay at three Fiordland National Park (FNP) huts along the way, and carry their own equipment and supplies. Today, approximately 10,000 or so guided and independent trampers tackle the track each year.

There is a down side to this as well. The area has some of the highest rainfall in the world, and though the rain may liven up the waterfalls, it doesn't do much for the views. The track is strictly regulated and must be walked in one of two groups of 40 people maximum, either as an independent walker or as part of the Milford Track Guided Walk (MTGW). Between November and April, you may walk in only one direction, from the Glade Wharf to Milford Sound, there is no camping, and you are allowed only one night in each hut. Well-manicured trails, litter regulations, mileage markers, buzzing sightseeing planes, and many buildings along the track combine to make it less than a true wilderness experience.

HISTORY

Maori lore indicates that a passage from the inland areas to Milford Sound was used for mining pounamu, New Zealand jade. The

Europeans who arrived in the region in the mid 1800s surprisingly learned nothing of this route and set out early on to find one.

Milford harbour was known to early seafarers in the mid-1800's. The first permanent European resident of Milford, Donald Sutherland, arrived by ship in 1877 and prospected the area. In later years, until his death in 1919, he played host to numerous travellers on the track. In 1881, he and John Mackay searched the Arthur Valley for minerals, coming across a magnificent waterfall now named for Mackay. Further up the valley, the immense three-tiered waterfall then thought to be the highest in the world, bears Sutherland's name. For many years he led increasing numbers of tourists up the valley to the base of the waterfall. After his discovery of the falls, Sutherland claimed to have discovered the pass into the Clinton Valley. At the time of his finding the pass, he said nothing of it, later claiming he didn't feel the route significant. The pass was the now famous Mackinnon Pass.

In 1888, Quintin Mackinnon and Ernest Mitchell accepted £30 to blaze a trail up the Clinton Valley from Lake Te Anau and search for an as yet undiscovered connecting passage to the sea. After weeks of bad weather, they turned back, and resupplied. They then ventured further up the valley to a lake, at the bottom of the pass, where a FNP hut now stands, and named it Mintaro or "resting place". They carried on and again in poor weather struggled over the pass that led to the Arthur Valley. Here they encountered Thomas Mckenzie, who from the other direction was also looking for an overland route to Te Anau. A rough track was finished in 1890. Quintin Mackinnon claimed discovery of the pass and became the track's first guide as the route from Te Anau to Milford was finally established. In 1892, Mackinnon died in a storm on Lake Te Anau. Sutherland, however, never recognized Mackinnon as the discoverer of the pass.

About the same time, in 1890, William Quill climbed to the top of the immense waterfall discovered several years previously by Donald Sutherland. Lake Quill, from which exits the waterfall ranked as the world's fourth highest, bears his name. Sutherland, however, claimed the right to give his name to the waterfall. Quill's feat is known to have been duplicated only once, in 1950 by a courageous track guide. Quill's own activities led to his death, also in 1890, when he fell while climbing.

In 1903, the government Tourist Department took over the track facilities, maintaining the Beech and Mintaro Huts built in the 1890s. Pompolona Hut, and Glade Hut were built and other buildings upgraded. A stone memorial was erected on the pass to honor Mackinnon, and the Beech Huts near the base of Sutherland Falls were renamed for Quintin. After years of trial and experience and many changes in the course of the track necessitated by flooding and heavy rains, a relatively stable course for the track was found.

Since there was no other route inland, a walk on the Milford track originally meant returning to Te Anau on the same track. In 1929, work was begun on the famous Te Anau - Milford Road. It took five years to blast the 1.3 kilometre tunnel at the Homer Saddle, with the cost of three lives, and the road did not open until 1954. At the conclusion of the trip, trampers now enjoy a boat ride across Milford Sound to Milford township where there are bus connections available to Te Anau. Finally, the establishment of Fiordland National Park in 1952 put the Milford Track in control of the Department of Conservation. In 1991, control of the Milford Track Guided Walk was taken over by Tourism Milford.

TRACK ACCESS

The Milford Track officially begins at Te Anau Downs, 34 kilometres north of Te Anau on the Milford Road, where the launch departs daily at 2 pm to the Glade Wharf. Included in the guided tour are the bus connections from Te Anau to Te Anau Downs, the launch at the end of the tramp from Sandfly Point to Milford, and the return bus from Milford to Te Anau. Independent walkers must book and pay for both the buses separately through Fiordland National Park Visitor Centre when making initial track bookings.

THE TRACK

For both groups, the trip begins with a 2 hour boat trip across Lake Te Anau from Te Anau Downs, on the S.S. Tarawera, the original launch built in 1899 to ferry walkers to the start of the Milford Track.

Lake Te Anau, the South Island's largest lake, on the eastern edge of Fiordland National Park, is surrounded by dense bush and jagged peaks, landscape as rugged as any in the world. At the Glade Wharf, trampers disembark and begin their moderate 53.9 kilometre journey.

The track may be walked in one direction only. You must stay one night in each hut and may not move onto the next hut. Time and distances are noted below in day-by-day sections, first for Milford Track Guided Walkers (MTGW), followed by those for Fiordland National Park (FNP) independent walkers. Guided walkers will spend the first night at Glade House, the second at Pompolona Hut, and the last night at Quintin Hut. The first day independent walkers will walk 8 kilometres to Clinton Forks Hut, 7 kilometres from Glade House. They spend the second night at Mintaro Hut, 4.4 kilometres from Pompolona, and the final night at Dumpling Hut, 3.2 kilometres from Quintin. For independent walkers, huts have gas rings, flush toilets, stoves for heat, and communal bunk rooms. Wardens, present at some of the huts, assist trampers with up-to-date information, weather and track conditions. Though the trip should not be taken lightly, it can be walked by anyone of average fitness. Rocky trails, poor weather, possible avalanche dangers and rising rivers can make the trip arduous.

GLADE WHARF (210m) to GLADE HOUSE (MTGW) (215m)
15 minutes, 1km

Elevation:	Almost level
Terrain:	Bush, riparian

GLADE WHARF (210m) to CLINTON FORKS HUT (FNP)
(250m) via GLADE HOUSE (MTGW) (215m)
2.00 hours, 8.4km

Elevation:	Almost level
Terrain:	Bush, riparian

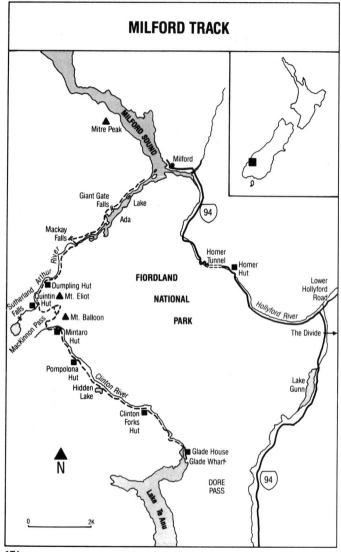

MILFORD TRACK

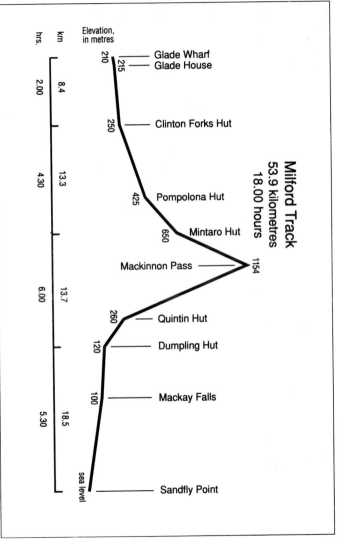

Disembarking from the launch at the Glade Wharf, you start out on the wide trail for the first kilometre through heavy forest to Glade House (MTGW). This first stop for guided hikers is located in a lovely clearing surrounded by mountains and the meandering Clinton River. Eels can be spotted here, and trout angling is excellent.

If you are an independent walker, you will soon put the buildings behind you as you cross a suspension bridge to the west side of the river. Following now on the true right of the river, you are quickly immersed in a heavy beech forest. The rest of the afternoon you spend easily ambling along the river on relatively flat ground. This wide trail, used as a means of resupplying the hut before helicopter service began in 1978, continues for 16 kilometres to the Pompolona Hut. At 3.5 kilometres, there is one good look back to Dore Pass, an extremely difficult high-level alternative route for experienced trampers to the track from the Milford - Te Anau Road. Four kilometres from Glade you'll pass through the moss-laden Black Forest, heavy with lichen and vines winding about. Clinton Forks Hut, 7 kilometres from Glade House, at the confluence of the North and West branches of the Clinton River (sleeps 40/gas/summer warden) consists of two separate buildings for trampers, and a new warden's residence, the old one having washed away in a 1989 flood.

GLADE HOUSE (MTGW) (215m) to POMPOLONA HUT (MTGW) (425m)
4.45 hours, 16.3km

Elevation:	Almost level
Terrain:	Bush, riparian

CLINTON FORKS HUT (FNP) (250m) to MINTARO HUT (FNP) (650m) via POMPOLONA HUT (MTGW) (425m)
4.30 hours, 13.3km

Elevation:	Almost level, parts moderate
Terrain:	Bush, riparian

After an hour along on the manicured track, at about the Six Mile Hut, the valley narrows, and the granite cliffs rise up steeply beside you. If rainfall is heavy, new waterfalls rise from its sheer sides, and snow might lace the upper edges of the cliffs. Soon you'll pass Hirere Falls and the MTGW lunch spot. About 2 kilometres after you reach a grassy scrub area, the Prairies, you get your first view north to Mackinnnon Pass and Mt Balloon (1853m). The flat pass rises abruptly from the bush below and you are provided an excellent preview of the next day's climb. A side track leads to Hidden Lake, known for its good swimming. It's 3 kilometres more to the Bus Stop, a covered FNP shelter, where the river crossing is often strewn with huge boulders, evidence of its susceptibility to flooding. In ½ kilometre you pass the turn off to Pompolona Hut, the second night for MTGW hikers. The original hut was washed away in a storm in October, 1986, and the new comfortable multi-tiered structure went up in only two months. Just beyond the hut, FNP hikers begin a steady 250 metre rise over the final 3.5 kilometres to Mintaro Hut (sleeps 40/gas/summer warden).

Strong FNP hikers with excess energy may wish to take advantage of fine weather and arrive at Mintaro early, leave their packs, and climb the additional 1½ to 2 hours to the pass. The weather changes so fast that sunshine now is no guarantee that pouring rain or low clouds won't obscure the view an hour later, or the following morning.

Here may be your first encounter with the famous kea, the world's only alpine parrot, "the clown of the mountains". Familiar in all alpine areas of the South Island, kea will dart down and grab anything unattached or shiny, or peck away at packs or loose clothing. Guard your equipment carefully. At Mintaro Hut several kea, hanging upside down from the roof, eyed me curiously, as I washed at the outside sink. One then swept in and carried away the washbasin stopper.

If you've some extra time, just beyond the turn-off to Mintaro Hut is a side track to the tiny Lake Mintaro, which was originally named by Mackinnon as the "resting place".

POMPOLONA HUT (MTGW) (425m) to QUINTIN HUT (MTGW) (260m) via MACKINNON PASS (1154m)
6.30 hours, 14.9km

Elevation:	Parts moderate, parts extremely steep
Terrain:	Bush, riparian
Special Features:	Mountain pass, mountain views, waterfall

MINTARO HUT (FNP) (650m) to DUMPLING HUT(FNP) (120m) via MACKINNON PASS (1154m)
6.00 hours, 13.7km

Elevation:	Extremely steep
Terrain:	Bush, riparian
Special Features:	Mountain pass, mountain views, waterfall

The most difficult and most exciting day lies ahead of you. You will climb from Mintaro Hut 360 metres and 5 kilometres to the top of Mackinnon Pass. After crossing the Clinton River via a swingbridge, you soon leave the soft moss covered forest and over the next 4 kilometres ascend the eleven zigzags to the top of the pass. The trail becomes noticeably rockier as you quickly emerge out into the harsh alpine environment above the treeline. Stop for a rest on one of the convenient rocks and admire the view back towards the Clinton Valley and Lake Mintaro. To the west are views of the Lady of the Snows. As you rise up to the top of the pass, you come to a large stone memorial which commemorates the European discovery of the pass by Quintin Mackenzie and Ernest Mitchell in 1888. The long narrow saddle straddles the land between Mt Balloon and Mt Hart, with precipitous drops down into its canyons on either side. The Jervois Glacier, north-east from the pass, is evident below the summit of Mt Elliot. You can also see straight down into the valley to Quintin Hut with its airstrip, 880 metres below at the foot of the Arthur Valley. In foul weather the pass is not a place to linger, but when skies are clear the views will never be forgotten! Continue on another kilometre (20 minutes) past numerous tarns to the Pass Hut.

Shared on one side by MTGW, the other by FNP, it's a fine place for a cuppa!

Leaving the warm shelter of the Pass Hut, begin the jarring descent on the main trail towards Mt Eliot. This steep and rocky section may be difficult for inexperienced trampers. At times of high avalanche danger on the main route, you will be instructed to use the emergency trail. One hour and 2¹/₂ kilometres drops you across the Roaring Burn, where there may be kea, and by the Crow's Nest, a former shelter. Finally back in the bush you descend across a swingbridge to Quintin Hut (MTGW) and the turn-off to Sutherland Falls. FNP walkers may leave their packs at the shelter for a side trip to the foot of the falls.

The side trip to Sutherland Falls, flowing from Lake Quill and falling from its edge to the ground in three giant leaps (1¹/₂ hours return), takes you to the base of the fourth highest waterfall (580m) in the world. The track to the deafening falls is rocky; unless you want a shower, keep away from the base. If the water level is right, you can walk behind the falls.

FNP trampers heading to Dumpling Hut (sleeps 40/gas/summer warden) should return again to Quintin and climb the Gentle Annie Hill back in the thick forest 3 kilometres, 1 hour to the hut.

QUINTIN HUT (MTGW) (260m) to SANDFLY POINT (sea level)
via DUMPLING HUT (FNP) (120m)
6.30 hours, 21.7km

Elevation:	Almost level
Terrain:	Bush, riparian
Special Features:	Waterfalls

DUMPLING HUT (FNP) (120m) to SANDFLY POINT (sea level)
5.30 hours, 18.5km

Elevation:	Almost level
Terrain:	Bush, riparian
Special Features:	Waterfalls

The last day out is a long one and you should get an early start in order to appreciate the scenery fully, and also to be on time for the launch. From Quintin, following the true right of the Arthur River, it's 10 kilometres (3 hours) back in the bush with the mountains high above you to the Boatshed, shelter for MTGW and FNP hikers. After a short rest, you cross the Arthur River on a swingbridge, arriving quickly at Bell Rock and the lovely multi-tiered Mackay Falls, named after one of the valley's early explorers. Crawl beneath the rock to explore the large space hollowed out by water.

Now on the true left of the river, the track crosses several footbridges until it reaches a view point that encompasses all of Lake Ada. Six kilometres (1½ hours) from Bell Rock, you'll find the rocks below roaring Golden Gate Falls a perfect spot for lunch and swimming. In case of rain, there is a shelter for both groups just before the swingbridge. It's another hour to the shelter at Sandfly Point (MTGW and FNP), where you can wait for the launch back to Milford. Since the Point is aptly named for its voracious sandflies, the shelters are well-used. Many will find a fine photo opportunity at the Sandfly Point 33 mile marker. Trampers should be aware that floods can cause delays especially after Dumpling Hut. If the track is closed, there is no boat service.

The launch trip, a quiet ending to the track, is a good time to reflect upon the last few days experience while gliding across the magnificent Milford Sound. From photographs you've seen, you'll no doubt recognize the famous Mitre Peak. Now you can answer the question for yourself: was this the finest walk in the world?

Launches at 2 and 3 pm transport trampers to Milford. FNP walkers wanting to take a boat tour of the Sound should take the 2 pm launch. Some will choose to spend the night in Milford and take in a boat tour of the Milford Sound the next day. Guided walkers will be escorted to the Milford Hotel for the night where they are booked for a celebration dinner, and a boat tour the next day.

ON YOUR OWN OR GUIDED?

Should you walk the track on your own or choose the guided trip?

Your decision should be based on your past experience, cost, level of fitness and personal preferences. Whichever you decide, you should book your trip six to eight months ahead.

Guided walkers (MTGW) carry only a day pack containing personal items like clothing, lunch, camera gear, etc. They lodge in comfortable dormitory style bunk rooms with food and bedding provided. Independent trampers should have previous tramping experience and be prepared to carry 15 kilograms of equipment and food. They stay in the more rustic FNP huts. Budget-conscious walkers may find the lower cost, which includes both launches, and hut fees, but not bus fares, more to their liking.

KEPLER TRACK

The Kepler Track, New Zealand's newest track starts and ends in Te Anau, at the base of the rugged Kepler mountain range. The well-maintained wide track offers splendid scenery and variety, passing from lake shore, through beech forests, across mountain tops in an alpine zone, before it drops back down into heavy bush laden forests.

HISTORY

Before the Europeans, Maori hunted and fished in the lower Kepler Mountains. Villages were built on the Waiau River and in Te Anau. In the 1880s, the Europeans used the eastern slopes of Mt Luxmore for farming sheep. Jack Beer settled an area west of the Waiau River, south of the Control Gates, where he grazed sheep. After his death in 1930 the land reverted to the National Park. In the 1970s there was a short-lived attempt to build a ski-field on Mount Luxmore.

Following environmental assessments, and several Government grants, construction began on a new track around the mountains in 1987. The new track was completed in 1988 during the National Park Centennial Year celebration.

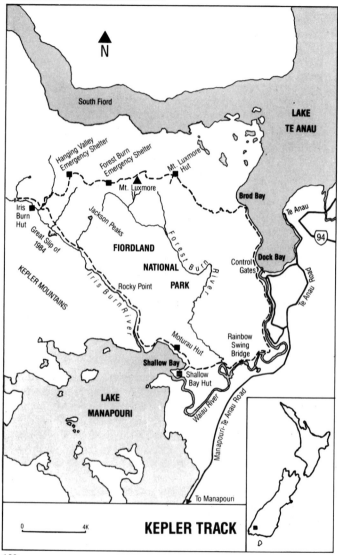

KEPLER TRACK

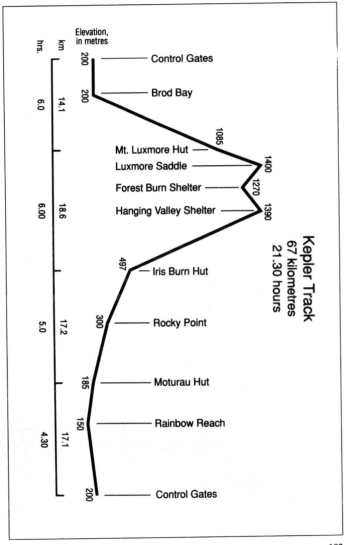

Kepler Track
67 kilometres
21.30 hours

Elevation, in metres

hrs.	km		
6.0	14.1	200	Control Gates
		200	Brod Bay
		1085	Mt. Luxmore Hut
6.00	18.6	1400	Luxmore Saddle
		1270	Forest Burn Shelter
		1390	Hanging Valley Shelter
5.0	17.2	497	Iris Burn Hut
		300	Rocky Point
4.30	17.1	185	Moturau Hut
		150	Rainbow Reach
		200	Control Gates

183

TRACK ACCESS

The track may be walked from Te Anau without use of transportation. However, Sinbad Cruises (booked through Fiordland Travel) will sail you across Lake Te Anau to Brod Bay, or Kepler Track Transport will take you to the Control Gates to begin the track. Pick-up may be arranged at the Waiau River swingbridge at the end. If you choose the sailing option the Control Gates to Brod Bay section is eliminated, and using the transport at the swingbridge end omits the level section along the Waiau River.

THE TRACK

The strenuous 67 kilometre track officially begins and ends at the Control Gates on Lake Te Anau, an hour's walk from the Visitor Centre (4.6km). Though the track may be walked in either direction, I'd advise starting with the Mt Luxmore section so you can put the heavy climb behind you on the first day, and be in the best position to assess the weather for the alpine crossing from Mt Luxmore Hut.

Gas rings and lighting, and flush toilets highlight three fully serviced modern huts. A warden is on duty during the more popular months. The section between Mt Luxmore Hut and Iris Burn should not be attempted in bad weather or high winds, and is not safe for small children. Camping is allowed only at Brod, Dock and Shallow Bays. Trampers should have previous experience as the walk is more physically demanding than the Milford, Routeburn, or Greenstone walks. Though the track is well-graded and nicely manicured, the days are long and there is a stiff 900 metre climb from Brod Bay to the Mt Luxmore Hut.

CONTROL GATES (200m) to BROD BAY (200m)
1.30 hours, 5.6km

Elevation:	Almost level
Terrain:	Bush, riparian
Special Features:	Lake views

After passing through the Control Gates, follow around the shore of

Luxmore Hut, Kepler Track

the lake 30 minutes to Dock Bay (camping). Crossing the Coal Creek swingbridge, continue around the lake 1 hour to the sandy beach at Brod Bay (camping), the usual stopping point for day hikers. You may stop for lunch and a dip, or if the hour is late it's a fine place to camp.

BROD BAY (200m) to MT LUXMORE HUT (1085m)
4.30 hours, 8.5km

Elevation:	Extremely steep
Terrain:	Bush, grassland
Special Features:	Mountain and fiord views

Immediately behind the picnic tables, the well-formed and sometimes steep track begins to climb in thick forest. Views of Lake Te Anau are glorious as the walk skirts its edge and then climbs up to Mt Luxmore. Stop for a breather at several viewpoints through the bush with views back to Te Anau. In 2 hours, at 747 metres you pass directly below steep limestone bluffs. In 2½ hours, you break completely out of the bush to an alpine tussock zone with fine views north to the Jackson Mountains. It's another 45 minutes through

185

open country to the spacious and comfortable Mt Luxmore Hut (sleeps 40/gas/summer warden) with its modern split-level design. There are splendid views of Lake Te Anau, across the South Fiord to the Murchison Mountains. You may wish to spend some of the evening exploring the limestone chambers in the Luxmore caves for stalagmite formations, calcium deposits on the bottom of the caves caused by dripping water.

MT LUXMORE HUT (1085m) to IRIS BURN HUT (497m) via MT LUXMORE SADDLE (1400m)
6.00 hours, 18.6km

Elevation:	Parts gradual, parts steep
Terrain:	Bush, grassland
Special Features:	Mountain and fiord views

This is a special day of walking across the mountain tops. If luck is with you, the weather will be fine. If not, you may experience high winds and rain on these exposed ridges. Strong winds make this ridge crossing dangerous for small children. You may wish to check with the warden for a weather report; and if the forecast is poor, wait out a day at Mt Luxmore. Be sure to carry water for the day's tramp.

From the Mt Luxmore Hut, the track begins a gradual 1 hour climb to the Mt Luxmore Saddle (1400m). You spend the next few hours on the mountain ridges with splendid views across the South Fiord to the Murchison Mountains and to Mt Irene. A short side trip to the summit of Mt Luxmore (1471m, 20 minutes return) adds a bit to the view. Another hour's gentle descent along the ridges finds you at the Forest Burn Emergency Shelter (1270m), the first of two modern prefabricated structures offering protection from high winds and rain on those undesirable days. The trail undulates again across the ridges another 2 hours to the Hanging Valley Emergency Shelter (1390m). It's another 2 hour descent to the hut, 30 minutes along the ridge to a view of the Iris Burn and the area of the Great Slip of 1984. Staircases have been built here to protect the fragile alpine environment. As you gradually enter the bush and descend

Iris Burn Hut, Kepler Track

in a series of zigzags, you drop steeply into the valley to the Iris Burn Hut (sleeps 40 / stove / summer warden) in a large tussock meadow. A 20 minute trip takes you to a lovely waterfall and swimming hole.

IRIS BURN HUT (497m) to MOTURAU HUT (185m)
5.00 hours, 17.2km

Elevation: Gradual
Terrain: Bush, riparian
Special Features: Lake views

This day's tramp follows the Iris Burn to Lake Manapouri at Shallow Bay. From the initial heavily forested section you climb a low saddle and emerge into a huge wasteland of jumbled rock across the valley floor, the site of the Great Slip of 1984. In about 2 to 2$^{1}/_{2}$ hours of gradual downhill you come to Rocky Point (300m), a small maintenance hut. Following the river, you enter a gorge and exit near the mouth at Lake Manapouri where fishing is good. A short walk around the edge of Shallow Bay takes you to Moturau Hut (sleeps 40/gas/summer warden), nicely situated at the lake's edge. Twenty minutes further around the bay you will come to Shallow Bay Hut (sleeps 6). Many trampers skip this hut and continue on the track to the Waiau River and pick up transport to Te Anau.

MOTURAU HUT (185m) to CONTROL GATES (200m)
via RAINBOW REACH (150m)
4.30 hours, 17.1 km

Elevation:	Almost level
Terrain:	Bush, riparian

Thirty minutes from the hut, you'll cross the sphagnum bog, a depression in the glacial moraine between Lake Manapouri and the Waiau River. The track skirts the Balloon Loop of the river and follows a terrace above the river. You can cross to an entry/exit point at the Rainbow Reach swingbridge, where trampers may meet the twice daily bus service to return to Te Anau. It's 12.6 kilometres to Te Anau on the Te Anau-Milford Highway. Continuing on the flat track, you'll encounter fine river views and good fishing all the way to the Control Gates, 10.9 kilometres from the swingbridge. You've now completed the loop you began several days ago. You may wish to meet the bus here or, if you got the time and energy, walk the extra 4.6 kilometres into Te Anau.

HOLLYFORD TRACK

The Hollyford Track traces a historic route along the northern section of Fiordland National Park below the Darran Mountains through bush to Martins Bay. This low-level track follows rivers and lake edges through heavy bush to greet seals and penguins at its northern coastal edge.

HISTORY

There is evidence that there was a seasonal Maori settlement at Martins Bay, but little was left of it in the 1860s when the Europeans explored the area. Tutoko and his daughters were one of the two families who remained in the area. Tutoko's name was given to the towering peak above the valley, the highest peak in Fiordland National Park. The first real knowledge of the Hollyford Valley came in 1861 when David McKellar and George Gunn viewed it from Key Summit. Two years later, Patrick Caples explored the valley, and a few months after that Captain Alabaster explored the valley from Martins Bay to Lake Howden.

Gold seekers established a settlement at Martins Bay at Jamestown in the mid-1800s. Difficulties were immediate, as no road was ever built down the Hollyford to the settlement, and ships with vital supplies had difficulty reaching the settlement. Their spirits broken by continued hardships, starvation, and isolation, the settlers had given up by 1878, and only a few people continued to live in Martins Bay. At the end of the 1870s, Donald Sutherland settled in nearby Milford and began his explorations of the Arthur Valley.

Through the years only the Mckenzie family, who raised cattle, remained at Martins Bay. In 1926 they sold their land to the Gunn family, Davy Gunn becoming a legend in the area. Until 1955 he brought travellers into the region on horse treks, and then his son Murray continued his operation. To this day, Murray Gunn, maintains a motor camp, store, and museum in Gunns Camp on the Lower Hollyford Road.

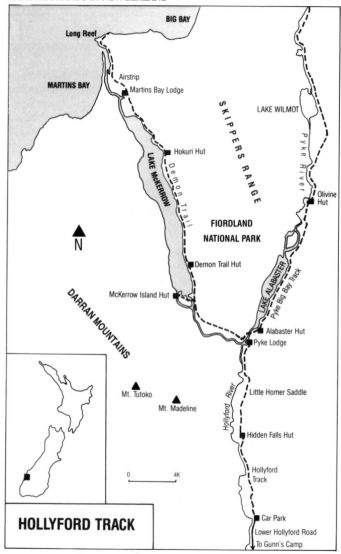

HOLLYFORD TRACK

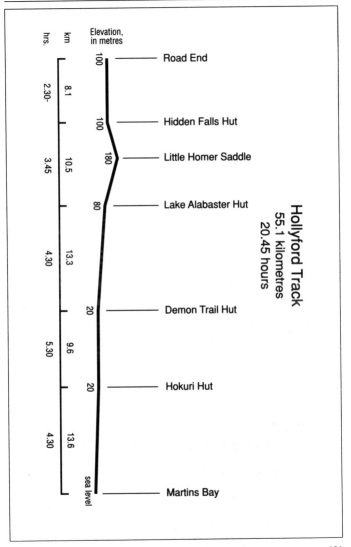

Hollyford Track
55.1 kilometres
20.45 hours

hrs.	km	Elevation, in metres	
		100	Road End
2.30-	8.1		
		100	Hidden Falls Hut
3.45	10.5	180	Little Homer Saddle
		80	Lake Alabaster Hut
4.30	13.3		
		20	Demon Trail Hut
5.30	9.6		
		20	Hokuri Hut
4.30	13.6		
		sea level	Martins Bay

By the end of World War II, the road into the Hollyford Valley went as far as Humboldt Creek, but it was feared that further extension would spoil the remote feel of this wild valley. In 1960, the area became part of Fiordland National Park and huts were built, bridges erected, and tracks upgraded.

TRACK ACCESS

The easiest way to reach the road end is by private car. The turn off to the Hollyford Road is located on SH 94 at Marian Corner, about one hour, 86 kilometres from Te Anau. InterCity, Mount Cook Landline or any of the other bus companies will leave you here, still 18 kilometres short of the track.

You should check at Fiordland National Park Visitors Centre in Te Anau for information on transport to the road end. The Hollyford Tourist and Travel Company runs a bus service from Te Anau to the road end, and Trip's 'n Tramps in Te Anau also offers service into the Hollyford Valley.

Hollyford Tourist and Travel Company offers a jet boat option between Rainbow Creek and Martins Bay. This is usually used to eliminate backtracking all of the track but the first day. You can also fly out from Martins Bay to Milford, Gunns Camp, or Queenstown with HTC or Air Fiordland, but flights are often grounded by poor weather.

THE TRACK

This 55.1 kilometre one way track takes four days from the Hollyford Road End to Martins Bay. You must backtrack back to the road end, or save several days with a fly-out or jet boat return. Though a low-level track with little elevation gain or loss, it gains a moderate rating due to its remote location, tricky river crossings and less-maintained trails.

HOLLYFORD ROAD END (100m) to
HIDDEN FALLS HUT (100m):
2.30 hours, 8.1km

Elevation: Almost level
Terrain: Bush, riparian
Special Features: Mountain views, waterfall

From the car park, an all-weather walkway sidles around some bluffs with spectacular views across the valley to the Darran Mountains. After 3 kilometres the track cuts through an open flat and passes Sunshine Hut, lunch stop for guided walkers. A few minutes farther along, Hidden Falls is located 2 minutes up from the track. Five minutes from here you'll find Hidden Falls Hut (sleeps 12/stove), with a good view of Mt Madeline.

HIDDEN FALLS HUT (100m) to LAKE ALABASTER HUT (80m)
via LITTLE HOMER SADDLE (180m)
3.45 hours, 10.5km

Elevation: Moderate
Terrain: Bush, riparian
Special Features: Mountain views

After 15 minutes, you begin a slow but steady climb for 40 minutes on well-maintained track to reach Little Homer Saddle, the high point of the track. Just before the saddle, a break through the trees affords a fine view of Mt Tutoko (2746m). From the saddle, the trail descends a steep switchback to a bridge over Little Homer Creek, and view of Little Homer Falls. In another 30 minutes, you reach a swingbridge over Rainbow Creek, at which point, the track becomes muddy and less well-maintained. Guided walkers may pick up a jet boat here, and be driven around this wet section. Independent walkers continue in bush until you reach Pyke Lodge (HTC) with some fine mountain views. In 15 more minutes, after passing the Pyke River Bridge, you reach Alabaster Hut (sleeps 20/stove) in a quiet spot on the lake shore.

LAKE ALABASTER HUT (80m) to DEMON TRAIL HUT (20m)
4.30 hours, 13.3km

Elevation: Almost level
Terrain: Bush, riparian

Retrace some of the previous day's steps to the Pyke River Bridge and cross to the rocky bluffs on the opposite side. This section of the track, in thick bush, makes for tough going. Views of the meandering river are limited. Crossing several creeks in heavy mud, under and over logs on overgrown track, may wear out the tramper. This difficult stretch may be by far the worst to be endured. With a bit of patience, you'll emerge in 3 hours at Lake McKerrow. A signed junction points the way across a channel to McKerrow Island and McKerrow Island Hut (sleeps 12/stove). Follow the track around the north of the island to the pleasant hut, but remember that if the channel rises after a heavy rain, you may be unable to leave the island.

The right junction joins the infamous Demon Trail. The track offers some hard going, in spots. Overall, however, the going becomes surprisingly easier when compared with the previous section. In 1^1/$_2$ hours, over two walkwires, you reach the modern Demon Trail Hut (sleeps 12/stove) on a terrace near Lake McKerrow.

DEMON TRAIL HUT (20m) to HOKURI HUT (20m)
5.30 hours, 9.6km

Elevation: Almost level
Terrain: Bush

Continue on the undulating track, remembering the worst is now behind you. You will have several walkwires to negotiate. Slowly you must pick your way through several slips which afford nice views of the lake, taking care here to look for markers as fallen rocks have obscured some of the track. The end of the Demon Trail brings you to the Hokuri Hut (sleeps 12/stove).

194

HOKURI HUT (20m) to MARTINS BAY, LONG REEF (sea level)
4.30 hours, 13.6km

Elevation:	Almost level
Terrain:	Bush, riparian
Special Features:	Tasman Sea; seal colony

Just after leaving the hut, you will have to negotiate Hokuri Creek which can be dangerous in high water. It might well be advisable to use the long walkwire 15 minutes upstream. The track then follows the lake shore for $1^1/2$ hours and passes the site of the old colony of Jamestown, of which little remains today of the settlement. In 30 minutes, you leave the lake and enter the muddy bush again.

After another hour more in bush you come to the open clearing of Martins Bay. There is a signpost to the Martins Bay Lodge (HTC) and airstrip, the main hut for the guided walkers. Stop here for a cuppa if you wish to make jet boat or plane reservations for your return trip. In 5 minutes you come to the turn-off to a private hut for trampers. Reservations for this hut or for return plane service may be made through Air Fiordland in Te Anau.

Continuing on through forest and over Jerusalem Creek, the track emerges from the bush near the old Martins Bay Hut. Once located in this lovely site overlooking the Bay above Long Reef, it unfortunately burned down in 1990. The reef has a special mysterious feel to it, and it's a fine place to while away an afternoon. Fifteen minutes along is a noisy, but appealing seal colony, sometimes with pups, and a rare penguin may also be seen. Continue on the cattle track to the east to Big Bay if you are planning the full Hollyford loop.

GUIDED TOURS

From October through April, the Hollyford Tourist and Travel Company (HTC) runs a variety of guided walks along the Hollyford Track. They maintain two lodges along the route, at lower Pyke and Martins Bay, provide home-cooked meals, bunk-room accommodation, showers and jet boat service around the track's difficult or muddy sections. Guided walkers (HTC) can chose to walk out, or weather permitting, fly out. HTC also runs the jet boat and air charter service for trampers, as well as a bus service to the start of the track. Trampers wishing to arrange for the jet boat or plane may call or write the HTC or drop by at their lodge at Pyke or Martins Bay.

OTHER

Continuing on the "Hollyford" loop from Long Reef to Big Bay (12.2km), Big Bay to Olivine (30.5km) and back to Alabaster (16.6km) requires an additional four to six days. The route is overgrown, huts are few and old, and rivers are not bridged. It should be attempted only by very experienced trampers.

CONTACTS:

Department of Conservation, Fiordland National Park Visitor Centre,
Box 29, Te Anau,   0-3-249 7921
Air Fiordland, Jailhouse Mall, Te Anau   0-3-249 7505
Fiordland Travel, P.O.Box 1, Te Anau,   0-3-249 7416
Kepler Track Transport , PO Box 81, Te Anau   0-3-249 7457
Sinbad Cruises, 15 Fergus Square, Te Anau   0-3-249 7106
    or   249 7416
Trips 'n Tramps, PO Box 69, Te Anau   0-3-249 7081
Visitor Information *(i)*, Milford Road, Te Anau   0-3-208 9908

TRACK BOOKINGS

Hollyford Track Bookings:

Hollyford Tourist and Travel Co. PO Box 205, Wakatipu, Central
    Otago,   0-3-442 3760

Milford Track Bookings:

Department of Conservation, Fiordland National Park Visitor Centre,
    Box 29, Te Anau (FNP independent walkers)

                                                     0-3-249 8514

Milford Track, Travel-lodge Te Anau, Box 185, Te Anau
    (MTGW guided walkers)   0-3-249 7411

APPENDIX
SUMMARY TABLES

Lake Waikaremoana Track

General Description:	Dense forests, plunging waterfalls, sweeping lake views, and good fishing in a remote area rich in Maori tradition characterize this tramp.
Total Kilometres:	51.1km
Time Required:	3-5 days
Average Total Walking Time:	20.30 hours
Rating:	Easy
Starting Elevation:	Hopuruahine Landing, 600m or Onepoto, 580m
Highest Point:	Panekiri Hut, 1180m
Base:	Aniwaniwa Visitor Centre
Maps:	Infomap 260 W18 Waikaremoana; Holidaymaker 239 Lake Waikaremoana
Huts:	Great Walks track

	Height in metres	Kilometres		Time	
		Sections	Total	Sections	Total
Hopuruahine Landing	600	0	0	0	0
Whanganui Hut	580	5.7	5.7	2.00	2.00
Te Puna Saddle	710	4.3	10.0	1.30	3.30
Te Puna Hut	580	1.3	11.3	.30	4.00
Te Kopua Saddle	690	5.0	16.3	2.00	6.00
Marauiti Hut	580	3.2	19.5	1.00	7.00
Whakaneke Spur	660	1.0	20.5	.30	7.30
Korokoro Falls Turn-Off	580	10.1	30.6	3.15	10.45
Waiopaoa Hut	580	2.5	33.1	.45	11.30
Panekiri Hut	1180	8.4	41.5	4.30	16.00
Onepoto	580	9.6	51.1	4.30	20.30

Round Mt Ngauruhoe Track

General Description:	This splendid circuit of Mt Ngauruhoe in Tongariro National Park provides a special tramping experience, passing through volcanic craters and near steaming emerald pools while traversing a moon-like landscape.
Total Kilometres:	49.5km
Time Required:	3-4 days
Average Total Walking Time:	20.00 hours
Rating:	Moderate

Starting Elevation:	Whakapapa Village, 1120m	
Highest Point:	above Red Crater, 1880m	
Base:	Whakapapa Village	
Maps:	Infomap 260 T19 Tongariro, S20 Ohakune, T20 Ruapehu;	
	Parkmap 273-04 Tongariro National Park	
Huts:	Great Walks track between Mangatepopo Hut and Ketetahi Hut (the Tongariro Crossing); all others Category 2	

	Height in metres	Kilometres		Time	
		Sections	Total	Sections	Total
Whakapapa Village	1120	0	0	0	0
Mangatepopo Hut	1190	9.0	9.0	3.00	3.00
Red Crater	1880	4.0	13.0	3.00	6.00
Emerald Lakes	1700	1.0	14.0	.30	6.30
Ketetahi Hut	1430	4.5	18.5	1.30	8.00
Emerald Lakes	1700	4.5	23.0	2.00	10.00
Oturere Hut	1350	5.0	28.0	1.30	11.30
New Waihohonu Hut	1120	8.0	36.0	3.00	14.30
Tama Saddle	1350	8.0	44.0	3.00	17.30
Whakapapa Village	1120	5.5	49.5	2.30	20.00

Round-the-Mountain Track (RMT)

General Description:	Circling Mt Egmont/Taranaki, this challanging high-level route offers expanansive views of the stunning volcano and surrounding plains.
Total Kilometres:	39.8km
Time Required:	3-4 days
Average Total Walking Time:	18.00 hours
Rating:	Strenuous
Starting Elevation:	Stratford Plateau, 1140m
Highest Point:	Punehu Stream, 1680m
Base:	New Plymouth
Maps:	Infomap 260 P20 Egmont;
	Parkmap 273-09 Egmont
Huts:	Category 2

	Height in metres	Kilometres		Time	
		Sections	Total	Sections	Total
Alpine (High Level)Variation					
Stratford Plateau	1140	0	0	0	0
Dawson Falls	900	2.0	2.0	1.0	1.0
Lake Dive Hut Turnoff	1300	6.0	8.0	2.30	3.30
Punehu Stream	1680	3.0	11.0	2.00	5.30
Waiaua Gorge Hut	610	3.7	14.7	2.30	8.00
Kahui Hut	880	5.5	20.2	2.30	10.30
High Point	1160	1.5	21.7	1.00	11.30
Holly Hut	975	6.1	27.8	2.00	13.30
Tahurangi Lodge	1520	8.0	35.8	3.15	16.45
Stratford Plateau	1140	4.0	39.8	1.15	18.00
Low Level Variation					
Dawson Falls	900	0.0	0.0	0.0	0.0
Lake Dive Hut	910	6.5	6.5	3.0	3.0
Taungatara Track	535	4.0	10.5	2.0	5.0
Waiaua Gorge Hut	610	5.5	16.0	3.0	8.0

Coast Track

General Description:	This scenic, easy walk on the north coast of the South Island is well-known for its sunshine, fine swimming and boating, and golden sand beaches.
Total Kilometres:	Marahau to Totaranui, 34km Totaranui to Wainui Inlet, 13km
Time Required:	3-5 days
Average Total Walking Time:	12 hours + 4.15 hours
Rating:	Easy
Starting Elevation:	Marahau, 5m
Highest Point:	Tonga Saddle, 120m
Base:	Nelson
Maps:	Infomap 260 N25 Tarakohe, N26 Takaka; Parkmap 273-07 Abel Tasman
Huts:	Great Walks track

	Height in metres	Kilometres		Time	
		Sections	Total	Sections	Total
Marahau	5	0	0	0	0
High Point	100	5.5	5.5	2.00	2.00
Torrent Bay	5	3.5	9.0	1.30	3.30
High Point	100	3.0	12.0	1.00	4.30
Falls River	5	1.0	13.0	.30	5.00

	Height in metres	Kilometres		Time	
		Sections	Total	Sections	Total
South Head Viewpoint	90	2.0	15.0	.45	5.45
Bark Bay	5	2.0	17.0	.45	6.30
High Point	120	1.0	18.0	.30	7.00
Tonga Quarry	5	1.0	19.0	.30	7.30
Tonga Saddle	120	4.5	23.5	1.30	9.00
Awaroa	5	4.5	28.0	1.00	10.00
Totaranui	5	6.0	34.0	2.00	12.00
Whariwharangi Bay	5	9.0	43.0	3.00	15.00
Wainui Inlet	5	4.0	47.0	1.15	16.15

Heaphy Track

General Description:	One of New Zealand's most popular tramps, this track crosses rolling tussock covered hills and parallels the pounding West Coast of the South Island.
Total Kilometres:	77km
Time Required:	4-5 days
Average Total Walking Time:	22.45 hours
Rating:	Easy
Starting Elevation:	Brown Hut, 122m or Kohaihai Shelter, sea level
Highest Point:	Flanagans Corner, 915m
Base:	Nelson or Karamea
Maps:	Infomap 260 M26 Cobb, L26 Heaphy; Trackmap 245 Heaphy
Huts:	Great Walks track

	Height in metres	Kilometres		Time	
		Sections	Total	Sections	Total
Brown Hu	122	0	0	0	0
Flanagans Corner	915	13.0	13.0	4.15	4.15
Perry Saddle Hut	868	3.0	16.0	.45	5.00
Gouland Downs Hut	610	8.0	24.0	2.00	7.00
Saxon Hut	670	6.0	30.0	1.45	8.45
High Point	750	5.0	35.0	1.30	10.15
James Mackay Hut	695	6.0	41.0	2.00	12.15
Lewis Hut	15	12.0	53.0	3.30	15.45
Heaphy Hut	5	8.0	61.0	2.30	18.15
Kohaihai Shelter	sea level	16.0	77.0	4.30	22.45

Wangapeka Track

General Description:	This rugged isolated bush walk, crosses North West Nelson State Forest Park, following the Wangapeka, Karamea and Little Wanganui River valleys.
Total Kilometres:	49.5km
Time Required:	4-5 days
Average Total Walking Time:	22.00 hours
Rating:	Strenuous
Starting Elevation:	Rolling River Junction Shelter, 300m
Highest Point:	Little Wanganui Saddle, 1087m
Base:	Nelson or Karamea
Maps:	Infomap 260 L27 Karamea, M28 Wangapeka; Trackmap 318 Wangapeka
Huts:	Helicopter, Stone: Category 3
	Kings Creek, Taipo, Little Wanganui: Category 2

	Height in metres	Kilometres		Time	
		Sections	Total	Sections	Total
Rolling River Shelter	300	0	0	0	0
Kings Creek Hut	460	9.5	9.5	3.30	3.30
Stone Hut	680	6.5	16.0	2.30	6.00
Wangapeka Saddle	1009	1.5	17.5	1.15	7.15
Helicopter Flat Hut	740	6.5	24.0	2.45	10.00
Taipo Bridge	580	2.5	26.5	1.30	11.30
Taipo Hut	700	5.5	32.0	2.00	13.30
Stag Flat Hut	945	1.5	33.5	1.00	14.30
Little Wanganui Saddle	1087	1.0	34.5	.30	15.00
Little Wanganui Hut	330	7.0	41.5	4.00	19.00
Road End	100	8.0	49.5	3.00	22.00

Travers-Sabine Loop Via Mt Robert

General Description:	Trampers visiting this rugged wild park meander through bush lined valleys connected by tarned alpine basins and rocky passes.
Total Kilometres:	64.5km
Time Required:	6-7 days
Average Total Walking Time:	33.30 hours
Rating:	Strenuous
Starting Elevation:	Lake Rotoiti, Kerr Bay, 630m
Highest Point:	Robert Ridge, 1850m
Base:	St Arnaud

| Maps: | Infomap 260 N29 St Arnaud, N30 Tarndale, M29 Murchison, M30 Matakitaki; Parkmap 273-05 Nelson Lakes |
| Huts: | Category 3, except for Angelus which is Category 2 |

	Height in metres	Kilometres		Time	
		Sections	Total	Sections	Total
Kerr Bay	630	0	0	0	0
Lakehead Hut	630	8.0	8.0	3.0	3.00
John Tait Hut	820	13.0	21.0	4.30	7.30
Uppers Travers Hut	1310	7.0	28.0	3.0	10.30
Travers Saddle	1768	2.0	30.0	1.30	12.00
West Sabine Hut	660	6.0	36.0	5.30	17.30
Sabine Hut	460	14.0	50.0	5.0	22.30
Mt Cedric	1532	3.0	53.0	2.30	25.00
High Point	1800	1.5	54.5	1.0	26.00
Angelus Hut	1650	2.5	57.0	2.30	28.30
Robert Ridge High Point	1850	.5	57.5	.30	29.00
Flagtop	1690	3.5	61.0	2.30	31.30
Mt Robert Car Park	880	3.5	64.5	2.00	33.30

Copland Track

General Description:	Trampers possessing the necessary skills will be richly rewarded by some of the most spectacular mountain scenery in New Zealand in this true alpine crossing of the Southern Alps.
Total Kilometres:	46km
Time Required:	3-4 days
Average Total Walking Time:	21.00 hours
Rating:	Expert
Starting Elevation:	Mount Cook Village, 730m
Highest Point:	Copland Pass, 2150m
Base:	Mount Cook Village
Maps:	NZMS 1 78 Bruce Bay, 79 Mt Cook
Huts:	Hooker: Category 1 Douglas Rock, Welcome Flat: Category 2

	Height in metres	Kilometres		Time	
		Sections	Total	Sections	Total
Mount Cook Village	730	0	0.0	0	0
Stocking Stream	800	4.0	4.0	1.15	1.15
Hooker Hut	1120	6.0	10.0	1.45	3.00

Copland Emergency Shelter	1830	2.0	12.0	4.00	7.00
Copland Pass	2150	1.0	13.0	1.00	8.00
Top of Zig-Zag	1220	3.0	16.0	1.30	9.30
Douglas Rock Hut	700	6.0	22.0	2.30	12.00
Welcome Flat Hut	425	7.0	29.0	3.30	15.30
Architect Creek	125	8.5	37.5	2.30	18.00
SH 6 - Road End	50	8.5	46.0	3.00	21.00

Routeburn Track

General Description:	The most spectacular of New Zealand's subalpine walks features views of the Darran Mountains and Hollyford Valley, and a crossing of the Harris Saddle.
Total Kilometres:	39km
Time Required:	2-3 days
Average Total Walking Time:	12.15 hours
Rating:	Easy
Starting Elevation:	The Divide, 532m, or Routeburn Shelter, 450m
Highest Point:	Bluffs above Harris Saddle, 1300m
Base:	Te Anau or Queenstown
Maps:	NZMS 1 122 Hollyford; Trackmap 335-02 Routeburn
Huts:	Great Walks track

	Height in metres	Kilometres		Time	
		Sections	Total	Sections	Total
Divide	532	0	0	0	0
Turn off to Key Summit	815	1.5	1.5	.30	.30
Lake Howden	700	1.5	3.0	.30	1.00
Earland Falls	1100	4.0	7.0	1.30	2.30
Lake Mackenzie	930	6.0	13.0	1.30	4.00
Harris Saddle	1237	10.0	23.0	3.30	7.30
High Point	1300	.5	23.5	.15	7.45
Routeburn Falls Hut	990	4.5	28.0	1.00	8.45
Routeburn Flats Hut	660	3.0	31.0	1.00	9.45
Routeburn Shelter	450	8.0	39.0	2.30	12.15
SIDE TRIPS: (round trip)					
To Key Summit	919		3.0	1.0	
To Conical Hill from Harris Saddle	1515		3.0	2.0	

Greenstone-Caples Track

General Description:	This loop trip features easy walking in two parallel valleys, a lovely tarned alpine pass, and fine angling in clear emerald green pools.
Total Kilometres:	69km (circular route)
	Greenstone Track alone: 36.5km
	Caples Track alone: 32.5km
Time Required:	4 days (2 + 2)
Average Total Walking Time:	21.30 hours
Rating:	Greenstone Track: easy
	Caples Track: moderate
Starting Elevation:	Greenstone Car Park, 330m
Highest Point:	Greenstone Track: north end of Lake McKellar, 660m
	Caples Track: McKellar Saddle, 945m
Base:	Queenstown
Maps:	NZMS 1 122 Hollyford, 131 Eglinton;
	Trackmap 335-02 Routeburn & Greenstone
Huts:	Category 2

	Time	Height in metres		Kilometres	
	Sections	Total		Sections	Total
Greenstone Car Park	330	0	0	0	0
Mid-Greenstone Hut	550	20.0	20.0	6.30	6.30
McKellar Hut	650	13.0	33.0	5.00	11.30
Junction of Tracks	660	3.5	36.5	1.00	12.30
McKellar Saddle	945	1.5	38.0	1.30	14.00
Upper Caples Hut	500	12.0	50.0	2.00	16.00
Mid-Caples Hut	400	9.0	59.0	2.30	18.30
Greeenstone Car Park	330	10.0	69.0	3.00	21.30

Rees-Dart Track

General Description:	This difficult tramp links the magnificent Rees and Dart valleys with a mixture of open grassy country and alpine scenery.
Total Kilometres:	76.5km
Time Required:	4-5 days
Average Total Walking Time:	27.00 hours
Rating:	Strenuous
Starting Elevation:	Muddy Creek, Rees Valley Road, 457m

	Highest Point:	Rees Saddle,1448m
	Base:	Queenstown
	Maps:	NZMS 1 113 Tutoko, 114 Earnslaw
	Huts:	Category 2

	Height in metres	Kilometres		Time	
		Sections	Total	Sections	Total
Rees Valley Road	457	0	0	0	0
Twenty-Five Mile Hut	533	6.5	6.5	2.0	2.0
Shelter Rock Hut	868	10.5	17.0	4.0	6.0
Rees Saddle	1448	5.0	22.0	3.0	9.0
Dart Hut	908	4.5	26.5	3.0	12.0
Daleys Flat	463	22.0	48.5	7.0	19.0
Paradise	393	28.0	76.5	8.0	27.0

Milford Track

General Description:	New Zealand's most famous tramp combines sections in dense bush with a visit to the world's fourth highest waterfall and a crossing over magnificent Mackinnon Pass.
Total Kilometres:	53.9km
Time Required:	4 days
Average Total Walking Time:	18.00 hours
Rating:	Moderate
Starting Elevation:	Glade Wharf, 210m
Highest Point:	Mackinnon Pass, 1154m
Base:	Te Anau
Maps:	NZMS 1 120 & 121 Bligh, 122 Hollyford; Trackmap 299 Milford
Huts:	Category 1

	Height in metres	Kilometres		Time	
		Sections	Total	Sections	Total
Glade Wharf	210	0	0	0	0
Glade House	215	1.0	1.0	.15	.15
Clinton Forks Hut	250	7.4	8.4	1.45	2.00
Pompolona Hut	425	8.9	17.3	3.00	5.00
Mintaro Hut	650	4.4	21.7	1.30	6.30
Mackinnon Pass	1154	4.0	25.7	3.00	9.30
Quintin Hut	260	6.5	32.2	2.00	11.30
Dumpling Hut	120	3.2	35.4	1.00	12.30
Mackay Falls	100	6.6	42.0	2.00	14.30
Sandfly Point	sea level	11.9	53.9	3.30	18.00

Kepler Track

General Description:	New Zealand's newest track, a loop trip through the Kepler Mountains from Te Anau, features well-maintained trails, new modern huts, and splendid views of the southern fiords.
Total Kilometres:	67km
Time Required:	3-4 days
Average Total Walking Time:	21.30 hours
Rating:	Strenuous
Starting Elevation:	Waiau Control Gates, 200m
Highest Point:	Mt Luxmore Saddle, 1400m
Base:	Te Anau
Maps:	Trackmap 335-09 Kepler; NZMS 1 149 Manapouri (track not on map)
Huts:	Great Walks track

	Height in metres	Kilometres		Time	
		Sections	Total	Sections	Total
Control Gates	200	0	0	0	
Brod Bay	200	5.6	5.6	1.30	1.30
Mt Luxmore Hut	1085	8.5	14.1	4.30	6.00
Luxmore Saddle	1400	2.5	16.6	1.00	7.00
Forest Burn Shelter	1270	3.0	19.6	1.15	8.15
Hanging Valley Shelter	1390	4.0	23.6	1.45	10.00
Iris Burn Hut	497	9.1	32.7	2.00	12.00
Rocky Point	300	8.0	40.7	2.30	14.30
Moturau Hut	185	9.2	49.9	2.30	17.00
Rainbow Reach	150	6.2	56.1	1.30	18.30
Control Gates	200	10.9	67.0	3.00	21.30

Side Trip to Mt Luxmore Summit (Round trip):

Mt Luxmore Summit	1471		1.0		.45

Hollyford Track

General Description:	This historic low-level track is known for its splendid bush, views of towering mountains, and seal and penguin colonies at Martins Bay.
Total Kilometres:	55.1km
Time Required:	4 days
Average Total Walking Time:	20.45 hours
Rating:	Moderate

Starting Elevation:	Hollyford Road End, 100m				
Highest Point:	Little Homer Saddle, 180m				
Base:	Te Anau				
Maps:	NZMS 1 105 Martins Bay, 113 Tutoko;				
	Trackmap 335-03 Hollyford				
Huts:	Category 3				

	Height in metres	Kilometres		Time	
		Sections	Total	Sections	Total
Road End	100	0	0	0	0
Hidden Falls Hut	100	8.1	8.1	2.30	2.30
Little Homer Saddle	180	4.5	12.6	1.15	3.45
Lake Alabaster Hut	80	6.0	18.6	2.30	6.15
Demon Trail Hut	20	13.3	31.9	4.30	10.45
Hokuri Hut	20	9.6	41.5	5.30	16.15
Martins Bay	sea level	13.6	55.1	4.30	20.45

PRINTED BY
CARNMOR PRINT & DESIGN, LONDON ROAD, PRESTON